FREE DVD  **FREE DVD**

Essential Test Tips DVD from Trivium Test Prep!

Dear Customer,

Thank you for purchasing from Trivium Test Prep! We're honored to help you prepare for your exam.

To show our appreciation, we're offering a **FREE** *Essential Test Tips* **DVD by Trivium Test Prep**. Our DVD includes 35 test preparation strategies that will make you successful on your big exam. All we ask is that you email us your feedback and describe your experience with our product. Amazing, awful, or just so-so: we want to hear what you have to say!

To receive your **FREE** *Essential Test Tips* DVD, please email us at 5star@triviumtestprep.com. Include "Free 5 Star" in the subject line and the following information in your email:

1. The title of the product you purchased.

2. Your rating from 1 – 5 (with 5 being the best).

3. Your feedback about the product, including how our materials helped you meet your goals and ways in which we can improve our products.

4. Your full name and shipping address so we can send your **FREE** *Essential Test Tips* DVD.

If you have any questions or concerns please feel free to contact us directly at 5star@triviumtestprep.com. Thank you!

– Trivium Test Prep Team

Table of Contents

Assessment and Diagnosis

Overview   -   -   -   -   -   -   -   -   -   5

Anatomy and Physiology   -   -   -   -   -   -   -   15

Pathophysiology   -   -   -   -   -   -   -   -   23

The Nursing Diagnosis-   -   -   -   -   -   -   -   45

Planning and Implementation

The Individualized Plan of Care   -   -   -   -   -   -   49

Pharmacology -   -   -   -   -   -   -   -   -   61

Evaluation

Care Plan Revisions   -   -   -   -   -   -   -   -   81

Education

The Education Plan   -   -   -   -   -   -   -   -   95

Professional Role Performance

The Nurse-Patient Relationship   -   -   -   -   -   -   113

Ethics and Professionalism   -   -   -   -   -   -   -   123

Practice Examination

Multiple-Choice Questions   -   -   -   -   -   -   -   135

Exclusive Trivium Test Prep Test Tips and Study Strategies

Study Strategies   -   -   -   -   -   -   -   -   208

Preparation Pointers -   -   -   -   -   -   -   -   209

Test Tips   -   -   -   -   -   -   -   -   -   210

Assessment and Diagnosis (16%)

Cardiovascular disease (CVD) is a global health issue. Cardiac/vascular (CV) nurses play major roles in reducing this serious worldwide global burden, as well as making significant contributions to enhance patient and community outcomes. Cardiac/vascular nurses need essential assessment and diagnostic skills, cardiovascular knowledge, and resources to enable them to be both leaders and mentors in cardiovascular disease management and prevention.

Overview

A cardiac/vascular nurse must possess excellent analytical and practical skills as well as knowledge of cardiovascular anatomy, physiology, and pathophysiology. They must be aware of various risk factors that affect the cardiovascular patient, as well as have extensive knowledge of various data collection procedures. These procedures include accurate and thorough patient histories, physical and diagnostic tests and tools, as well as clinical findings provided by other medical professionals. Cardiac/vascular nurses must be capable of assessing, interpreting and synthesizing gathered information as it pertains to cardiovascular patients.

Cardiac/Vascular Patient History

Health History

When performing an accurate, thorough assessment of a cardiovascular patient, the first step is to obtain a health history. After introducing yourself and explaining what will take place during the course of the health history and physical exam, inquire about the patient's chief complaint. A basic CV physical assessment will include the following observations and/or measurements:

- Temperature
- Blood pressure
- Pulse
- Respirations
- Body weight and height
- Skin assessment
- Extremity assessment

- Fingernail assessment

- Head movement assessment

- Eye assessment

- Cardiac and vascular assessment

The cardiovascular patient's personal and family health history are also very important to note. Personal and/or family cardiovascular history items to take note of include the following:

- Hypertension

- Myocardial infarction (MI or heart attack)

- High cholesterol levels

- Coronary artery disease (CAD)

- Diabetes

- Smoking

- Alcohol consumption – low, moderate, heavy

- Amount/type of exercise

- Diet (in the last 24 hours to establish typical eating habits)

- Any changes in color/temperature of extremities

- Any history of leg pain when walking

- Any history of leg sores that do not heal

- Any history of blood clots

Common Chief Cardiovascular Complaints

Cardiac/vascular patients may present with several problems. Their chief complaint may include one of the following signs and/or symptoms:

Chest Pain

Many C/V patients will complain about chest pain at some point in time. Initially, the cause may be difficult to ascertain. Often, chest pain is precipitated and/or aggravated by things like anxiety, stress, deep breathing, exertion, and/or eating certain types of food. Chest pain can be characterized as:

- Sudden or gradual onset

- Radiating to the arms, back, neck, and/or jaw

- Intermittent or steady

- Mild or severe

- Sharp, shooting sensation

- Feeling of fullness and/or heaviness

- Feels like indigestion

PQRST

Utilizing the PQRST memory mnemonic tool helps in the assessment of a cardiovascular patients' chest pain. It allows them to describe their pain in more detail. Always keep possible emergency care in mind based on the severity of the patient's chest pain:

- **P (P**rovocative or **P**alliative) – What makes the chest pain worse or better?

- **Q (Q**uantity or **Q**uality) – How does the pain feel? Experiencing at the time of the examination? More/less severe than usual? How does it affect normal activities?

- **R (R**adiation or **R**egion) – Where in the chest is the pain located? Does it move to other areas as well?

- **S (S**everity) – How does the patient rate the pain on a scale of 0 to 10 with 10 being the most severe? Does it seem to reduce, intensify or same more or less the same?

- **T (T**iming) – When did the pain start? Did it come on suddenly or gradually? Frequency of the pain? Duration?

Palpitations

Typically felt over the precordium (area of chest wall overlapping the great vessels and heart) and/or throat/neck area, palpitations are generally defined as a conscious perception of the heartbeat. While many palpitations are insignificant, they can be the result of cardiovascular disorders such as high blood pressure, arrhythmias, mitral prolapse, and mitral stenosis. Palpitations can be characterized as:

- Regular or irregular
- Slow or fast
- Sustained (continuing) or paroxysmal (a severe attack or sudden increase in level of intensity)

Syncope

Usually occurring abruptly and lasting for several seconds to minutes, syncope is defined as a brief loss of consciousness, which occurs due to lack of oxygen to the brain. It can be caused from disorders such as aortic stenosis, aortic arch syndrome, and/or arrhythmias. Signs and symptoms of syncope may include:

- Lying motionless
- Relaxed skeletal muscles
- Pallor
- Weak, slow pulse rate
- Low blood pressure
- Breathing, which is almost impossible to detect

Intermittent Claudication

Intermittent claudication is defined as severe, cramping type pain of the limbs caused by exercise. This pain subsides after a few minutes of rest. Typically occurring in the legs, it can be either an acute or chronic problem. If it is an acute condition, it can signal acute arterial occlusion (blockage) that stems from disorders such as arteriosclerosis obliterans (narrowing and gradual blockage of the artery) or aortic arteriosclerotic occlusive disease.

Ask the following probing questions when enquiring about a patient's intermittent claudication:

- How far can you walk without any pain and/or cramping occurring?
- How long does the pain/cramping take to subside upon resting?
- Do you need to rest more frequently than you did before?
- Is the pain-rest pattern variable?
- How does this particular symptom affect your overall lifestyle?

Peripheral Edema

Peripheral edema is swelling of the arms and/or legs as the result of excessive interstitial fluid within the tissues. Edema of the arms can be caused by superior vena cava syndrome (direct blockage of the superior vena cava often caused by malignancies) or thrombophlebitis (inflammation or swelling of a vein resulting from a blood clot).

Leg edema can signal cardiac/vascular conditions such as chronic venous insufficiency, thrombophlebitis, and right-sided heart failure. Ask the following probing questions when enquiring about a patient's peripheral edema:

- How long have you noticed the swelling and inflammation in your limb(s)?
- Did your edema come on slowly or instantaneously?
- Does the swelling improve if you elevate the affected extremity?
- When is it at its worst (e.g. first thing in the morning or as the day goes on)?
- Have you recently been immobilized by either an injury and/or surgical procedure to the affected limb? Immobilized by another type of illness?
- Do you take any over-the-counter and/or prescription medications?
- Do you or a member of your immediate family have a previous history of C/V disease?

Risk Factors

Cognitive Impairment

In the acute clinical care setting, cardiac/vascular patients are at an increased risk for cognitive changes. This may be the result of both their illness and associated treatments. Impairment in cognition can lead to many problems including:

- Difficulties in communicating with others

- Personal safety risks, such as falls

- Limitations in self-care and activity levels as a result of fatigue, weakness, or other

- Inability to take part in personal care decisions

- Behavioral issues

As part of a complete patient assessment, the CV nurse is responsible for performing cognitive assessment of cardiac/vascular patients utilizing critical judgment as well as standardized cognitive assessment tools. Early assessment and intervention can have a significant effect on the cardiac/vascular patient's future prognosis and outcome.

Changes in cognition can be warning signals of acute, critical and/or life-threatening conditions. These include:

- Alcohol/drug withdrawal or toxicity

- Systemic infections

- Stroke

- Renal failure

- Fluid and/or electrolyte imbalance

- Embolus

The cognitive abilities of a cardiac/vascular patient can be assessed using a brief, bedside questionnaire known as the Mini-Mental State Examination (MMSE):

- Level of consciousness: Responds to own name? Alert? Drowsy? Fluctuating in consciousness level? Stuporous? Comatose?

- Orientation: Appropriate awareness of person, place, time and situation?

- Attention: Able to repeat short sentences as spoken to them?

- Concentration: Able to spell short word backwards?

- Memory: Can remember both recent and past information?

- Language: Fluent speech? Incoherent? Rambling? Repeating same word(s) or phrase(s) over and over?

- Thought processes: Delusional? Suicidal thoughts?

- Perception: Understands current environment?

Physical Disabilities

In the United States, approximately 1.5 million heart attacks and strokes occur every year. Cardiac/vascular diseases such as heart disease and stroke are the leading causes of death, resulting in one out of every three deaths. While both heart disease and stroke can be fatal, they can also lead to serious illness, disability, and reduced quality of life. Heart disease and stroke are two of the leading causes of disability in America, and approximately 3 million persons have some form of disability from these conditions.

Strokes often cause significant disability including complete or partial paralysis, speech impairment, and emotional or psychological issues. After suffering a heart attack, many cardiac patients experience various degrees of fatigue and depression. Additionally, cardiac/vascular patients sometimes find it difficult to engage in their normal physical activities.

Heart disease and stroke are very expensive health problems. Combined, these conditions account for around 12 billion dollars in lost productivity and healthcare expenditures every year. Typically, families who have an immediate family member who suffered from a stroke and/or heart disease have to content with both huge medical bills as well as lost earnings. There is also the distinct possibility of families experiencing a decreased standard of living.

A cardiac/vascular nurse is required to observe, recognize, assess, and report any physical and/or mental disabilities in their patients. As a result, they must develop and implement an individualized nursing care plan, provide the necessary level of patient care, and exercise the appropriate level of sensitivity to the cardiac/vascular patient.

Analytic Tools

Possessing analytical skills means having the ability to visualize, articulate, and solve both uncomplicated and complex problems and/or concepts. Taking the gathered data and/or available information one formulates sound, sensible decisions. CV nurses must be able to demonstrate that they have the necessary analytical skills to effectively apply logical thinking with respect to data pertinent to the cardiovascular patient.

Using various analytic tools, a cardiac/vascular nurse analyzes the gathered information, designs solutions to patient problems and formulates appropriate patient care plans. Two analytic tools that are useful for assessing levels of pain and perceived exertion include the pain scale and the Borg scale.

Pain Scale

Pain is a subjective experience expressed by an individual at any given time. Many medical professionals consider it to be the fifth vital sign, to go along with temperature, pulse, respirations, and blood pressure. Effective pharmacotherapy depends on an accurate pain assessment. Numerical scales can assist in a patient's perception of their level of pain. The following pain scale can be utilized by a cardiac/vascular nurse and patient in effective pain management.

- 0 – pain free

- Mild 1 – faint, slight, barely noticeable

- Mild 2 – little, light, uncomfortable

- Mild 3 – not bad

- Moderate 4 – disturbing

- Moderate 5 – moderate

- Moderate 6 – frightful

- Severe 7 – alarming, severe, awful

- Severe 8 – horrendous, agonizing

- Severe 9 – intolerable, excruciating, extreme

- Severe 10 – unspeakable, gut-wrenching

Borg Scale

Known as the Borg Rating of Perceived Exertion (RPE) or simply the Borg Scale, this is a tool that can be used to measure levels of intensity related to physical activity. Perceived exertion is defined as how hard a person feels their body is performing at a specific time. It depends on factors such as sensations experienced during periods of physical activity (elevated respirations, elevated heart rate, increased level of sweating, muscle fatigue, etc.) While this is a subjective method of measurement, a patient's perceived rating of exertion can provide a relatively accurate estimation of the actual heart rate during periods of physical activity.

Ranging from 6 (no exertion) to 20 (maximum exertion), patients make use of this scale in order to assign numbers to the way they feel while exerting themselves. Medical practitioners generally agree that perceived exertion ratings of 12 to 14 on the Borg Scale indicate that a moderate intensity level of physical activity is being performed.

There is a high correlation between a patient's rating of perceived exertion, multiplied by a factor of 10, and their heart rate during physical activity. Hence, a perceived exertion rating can give quite a good estimate of actual heart rate during a period of activity (e.g. if the Borg Rating of Perceived Exertion is 12, the heart rate should be around 10 x 12 = 120 beats per minute). It is important to note that actual heart rates can vary significantly based on a patient's age and physical condition.

The RPE is the preferred assessment method for measuring the intensity of physical activity in those patients who take medications affecting heart and pulse rates. The Borg Rating of Perceived Exertion is described below:

6 - No exertion of any kind

7 - Extremely light exertion

8

9 - Very light exertion (e.g. walking slowly for several minutes)

10

11 - Light exertion

12

13 - Somewhat hard exertion but still able to continue

14

15 - Hard (heavy) exertion

16

17 - Very hard exertion or strenuous (can still continue, very tired, and have to push)

18

19 - Extremely strenuous exertion (the greatest exercise level ever performed)

20 - Maximal exertion

The Quality of Data

Quality healthcare for any patient relies on the availability of accurate data. Inaccurate data, poor documentation, and insufficient communication can lead to adverse incidents, serious errors, and even death. Inaccurate data threatens the safety of all patients, potentially resulting in increased costs, inefficiencies, and/or poor financial performance of the institution. In addition, insufficient and inaccurate data hinders the exchange of health information and inhibits clinical research, performance improvement, and initiatives related to quality measurement.

A patient's complete electronic health record (EHR) is an example of accurate, appropriate medical health content, which is available in a usable, accessible format. It can:

- Improve the healthcare professional's ability to provide evidence-based management of the patient.
- Have a positive impact on quality of care, patient safety and/or staff/hospital efficiencies

Cardiac System

Located underneath the sternum (breastbone) and within the mediastinum (cavity containing the organs and tissues separating the two pleural sacs of the lungs), the heart is a hollow muscular organ. It is about the size of an adult's fist and weighs between 10 and 14 ounces.

Heart Layers

The heart is made up of several layers and structures. These include:

- *Epicardium*: Outer heart surface which consists of squamous epithelial cells over top of connective tissue

- *Myocardium*: Middle layer which makes up the majority of the heart wall. The thickest and strongest layer, it is made up of striated muscle fibers which cause heart contractions

- *Endocardium*: Innermost layer that lines the heart chambers. It is composed of endothelial tissue with smooth muscle bundles and small blood vessels

- *Pericardium*: A membranous sac, referred to as the pericardium, surrounds the heart as well as the roots of the great vessels. The apex is the narrow, bottom part of the heart, and it is the location where the heart sounds are heard the best

Heart Chambers

- *Right Atrium* – Upper right chamber which receives deoxygenated blood from the lower part of the body via the inferior vena cava. The right atrium receives deoxygenated blood from the head, neck, and arms via the superior vena cava. Additionally, it serves much like a reservoir for blood, which leaves this chamber and goes into the right ventricle.

- *Left Atrium* – Upper left chamber which receives oxygenated blood, which is delivered by the pulmonary veins from the lungs. It also acts as a reservoir for blood that is sent down into the right ventricle.

- *Right Ventricle* – Lower right chamber which receives deoxygenated blood from the right atrium. Acts as one of the heart's major "pumping stations" sending blood to the lungs via the left and right pulmonary arteries.

- *Left Ventricle* – Lower left heart chamber which gets oxygenated blood from the left atrium. It also serves as the heart's major "pumping station," as it sends blood to all body parts by way of the aorta.

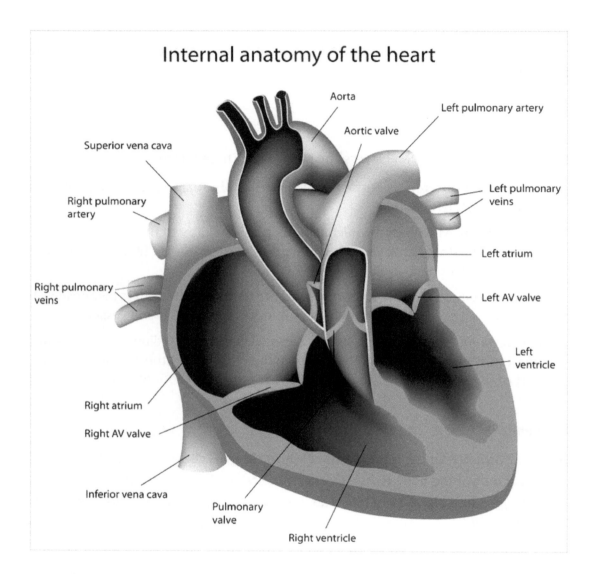

Internal anatomy of the heart

Heart Structures

- *Interatrial Septum* – This is a muscular partition that divides the chambers of the atria, and helps the chambers contract, forcing blood down into the ventricles.
- *Interventricular Septum* – This structure separates the two ventricles, and it assists in pumping blood.

- *Papillary Muscles* – Found within the ventricular walls, these muscles form a tight seal in order to stop backflow when the ventricles contract.

Heart Valves

The heart also contains four valves which allow forward blood flow through the heart and stop backward flow of blood. These are:

- *Mitral (bicuspid) Valve* – This stops backflow of blood from the left ventricle into the right atrium).
- *Tricuspid Valve* – This prevents backflow from the right ventricle up into the right atrium) valves.
- *Aortic Valve* – This prevents backflow from the aorta into the left ventricle.
- *Pulmonic Valve* – This stops backflow of blood from the pulmonary artery into the left ventricle).

Changes in pressure within the heart affect the opening and closing of these valves. The degree of contraction of the chamber as well as the amount of blood stretching it determines the pressure.

Vascular System

The vascular system is made up of two types of large vessels – arteries and veins.

Arteries

The arteries are large vessels which deliver oxygen-rich blood from the heart to other areas of the body. These vascular structures have muscular, thick walls in order to handle the high pressure and speed of blood flow. They include:

- *Aorta* – This is the largest artery in the body, and it is made up of the ascending aorta, aortic arch as well as the thoracic and abdominal portions of the descending aorta.
- *Collateral arteries* –These act as connections between two arterial branches.
- *Arterioles* – These structures are tiny, thinner arterial branches that deliver blood to body tissues and control the flow of blood to the capillaries.
- *Capillaries* – These vessels are tiny blood vessels with microscopic walls that join arterioles and venules.

Types of Arteries

Arteries can be classified further by their function. Two types are:

- *Conductive arteries* – Such as the external iliac artery, generally have few branches and follow fairly straight lines.

- *Distributive arteries* – These have multiple branches that spread out from the conductive arteries.

Veins

Veins possess thinner but larger diameter walls than arteries because of low pressure venous return. They take deoxygenated blood from the capillaries and transport it back to the heart for re-oxygenation. The largest vein in the body is the vena cava which returns blood to the right atrium, and it contains no valves.

Valves located within the veins prevent the backflow of blood. The majority of valves are found in smaller distal veins. The coronary sinus is the largest coronary vein, and its function is to return deoxygenated blood from the myocardium to the right atrium. Venules have thinner walls than the arterioles and they gather blood from the capillaries.

Flow of Blood through the Heart

Blood flows through the heart in three separate steps.

1. Blood fills the chambers: As mentioned above, the right atrium receives deoxygenated blood from the body via the superior and inferior venae cava. It also receives blood from the heart by way of the coronary sinus. The left atrium gets oxygenated blood from the lungs through four pulmonary veins. Passive ventricular filling starts with diastole.

2. Atria contract and remaining blood enters into ventricles: The two atria pump their blood, through the mitral (bicuspid) and tricuspid valves, directly into their respective ventricles.

3. Ventricles contract and blood goes into aorta and pulmonary arteries: The right ventricle pumps blood into the pulmonary arteries through the pulmonic valve and returns it to the lungs. After oxygenation, this blood returns to the left atrium, thus completing pulmonic circulation.

Blood Flow in Human Circulatory System

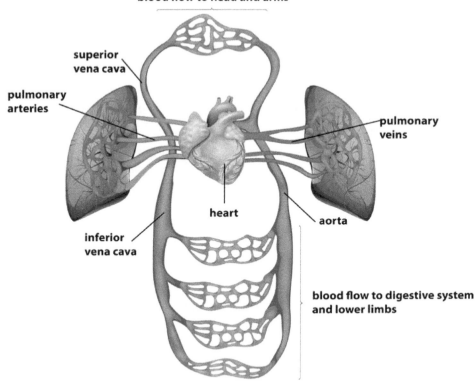

Cardiac Blood Flow Mnemonic

A useful mnemonic (memory tool) to remember cardiac blood flow is BB-RR-LLL.

>   **B** - Barren
>
>   **B** - Blood
>
>   **R** - Returns on the
>
>   **R** - Right
>
>   **L** - Loaded Blood
>
>   **L** - Leaves on the
>
>   **L** - Left

Cardiac Conduction

Within the right atrium there are two nodes known as the sinoatrial (SA) and the atrioventricular (AV) nodes. The SA node (pacemaker) is located in the upper portion of the right atrium just below the superior vena cava opening, and it initiates and regulates the heartbeat. The AV node, located in the right atrium base, slows impulses allowing the atrium to complete contraction and the ventricle to fill with blood. The SA node has a firing rate of 60 to 100 hundred beats per minute while the AV node's rate of firing is 40 to 60 beats per minute.

Cardiac conduction begins with the pacemaker (SA node). An impulse leaves the SA node, travels through the atria along the strand of fibers known as the Bachmann's bundle and intermodal pathways, on its way to the AV node. After passing through the AV node, the impulse travels to the ventricles. First, it passes through the Bundle of Hiss, then along the smaller bundle branches downwards to the Purkinjee fibers, causing contractions of the ventricle.

Four Characteristics of Cardiac Cells

- Automaticity - Able to spontaneously initiate an impulse (e.g. pacemaker cells)
- Excitability – Ability to respond to an electrical impulse. This results from an ion shift across the cell membrane
- Conductivity – Able to spontaneously transmit an electrical impulse to another cardiac cell
- Contractibility – Ability to contract and shorten after receiving an electrical impulse from another cell

De-Polarization and Re-Polarization Cycle

While impulses are being transmitted, heart cells undergo what are referred to as de-polarization and re-polarization cycles. When the heart is at rest, and no electrical activity is occurring, it is in a polarized state. However, negative charges flow, which disturbs the resting state. Since the heart has the ability to react in this state, it is said to have resting potential. When disturbed by an impulse from the SA node, ions flow into the cardiac muscle. This action results in the heart possessing action potential and the cells become de-polarized. Then, the heart attempts to return to its resting state by balancing negative ions with positive ions. The heart is trying to become re-polarized again.

There are five stages to the cycle:

- Phase 0: Rapid de-polarization – sodium moves into the cell rapidly – calcium moves into the cell slowly.
- Phase 1: Early Re-polarization – sodium channels close.
- Phase 2: Plateau – calcium continues to flow into the cell – potassium flows out.
- Phase 3: Rapid re-polarization – calcium channels close – potassium flows out quickly.

- Phase 4: Resting phase – active transportation through sodium-potassium pump starts to restore potassium to the inside and sodium to the outside of the cells – cell membrane becomes impermeable to sodium – potassium may move out of the cells.

Cardiac Output

Cardiac output refers to the quantity of blood ejected by the heart in one minute, measured in liters. Typically, cardiac output measures anywhere from 4 to 8 liters per minute.

Formula to Measure Cardiac Output

To measure cardiac output, take the heart rate and multiply it by the stroke volume (i.e. amount of blood ejected with each ventricular contraction). Stroke volume is usually 60 to 100 ml. and depends on three separate factors, namely preload, contractibility, and afterload.

- Preload: Quantity of blood still in the ventricle at the end of diastole (i.e. relaxation). This is the period of time between contraction of the ventricles or atria when blood enters into the relaxed chamber).
- Contractibility: Inherent ability of the muscular myocardium to contract normally.
- Afterload: Amount of pressure ventricular muscles must generate in order to overcome higher pressure within the aorta to eject blood from the heart.

Cycle of Heart Sounds

When a nurse auscultates a cardiac/vascular patient's chest with a stethoscope, he or she will hear sounds commonly known as "lubs" or "dubs". These are the first and second heart sounds, also referred to as S1 and S2.

These heart sounds are produced by the events of the cardiac cycle, which is the period of time from the beginning of one heartbeat to the beginning of the next heartbeat. As valves close or blood fills the ventricles, the heart muscle vibrates, which can be heard through the chest wall.

Basically, the cardiac cycle is made up of two separate phases, systole and diastole.

- Systole: AV valves close preventing backflow into the atria > atria relax > ventricles contract > long, low pitched S1 or "lub" sound occurs.

- Diastole: SL valves close preventing backflow into the ventricles > atria contract > ventricles relax > short, sharp pitched S2 or "dub" sound takes place

Pathophysiology

Heart Failure (HF)

The heart is "too pooped to pump." Often referred to as Congestive Heart Failure (CHF), this cardiac condition was renamed in 2005. It is defined as an inability of the heart to pump adequate amounts of blood to meet the body's demands. Heart failure is characterized by decreased cardiac output resulting from impaired contractile properties of the cardiac muscle, which is myocardial performance with an ejection fraction (EF) < 35-40%.

Right-Sided Heart Failure

Right-sided heart failure is due to ineffective contraction of the right ventricle. It can be caused by either a pulmonary embolus or an acute right ventricular infarction. However, profound backward flow of blood as a result of left-sided heart failure is the most common cause.

Signs and Symptoms of Right-Sided Heart Failure

- Edema, initially located in a dependent area
- Distention of the jugular vein
- Hepatomegaly (abnormal liver enlargement)
- Ascites (accumulation of fluid in the peritoneal cavity)
- Weakness
- Nausea and vomiting
- Decreased urinary output
- Generalized gain in weight

Left-Sided Heart Failure

Left-sided heart failure is the most common type. It is often caused by valve disease, pulmonary hypertension, chronic obstructive lung disease (COPD), or acute respiratory distress syndrome (ARDS). The symptoms of left-sided failure result from increased intravascular volume caused by reduced cardiac output and its effects on perfusion of the kidneys. Decreased renal perfusion leads to elevated aldosterone secretion, retention of fluid and sodium plus increased intravascular volume.

Signs and Symptoms of Left-Sided HF

- Cough

- Tachycardia (increased pulse)

- Dyspnea (shortness of breath), initially on exertion

- Anxiousness

- Muscle weakness

- Fatigue

- Pallor or cyanosis (bluish skin discoloration)

- Bibasilar crackles (rattles made by one or both lungs)

Risk Factors of Left-Sided HF

- Hypertension

- Coronary artery disease

- Myocardial infarction

- Congenital heart disease

- Cardiac infections

- Substance abuse in patients over 65 years of age

- Diagnostic Evaluation of HF

- Complete history and physical examination (H &P)

- Chest x-ray (CXR)

- Laboratory tests

- Electrocardiogram (ECG)

- Echocardiogram

- Arterial blood gases (ABGs)

- Monitoring of pulmonary artery pressure

- Brain (beta-type) natriuretic peptide (BNP) – Inexpensive blood test to assist in the determination of a treatment plan. With this, < 100, HF is mild, 100-400, HF is moderate, and > 400, HF is definite or severe

Objectives of Medical Management of HF

- Promoting rest to decrease work load on the heart
- Increasing efficiency/force of the contractions of the myocardium
- Eliminating excess accumulation of edema fluid
- Improving functional capacity
- Relieving heart failure symptoms
- Improving quality of the patient's life
- Decreasing the chances of mortality

Medical Interventions and Treatments for HF

Early detection and treatment of the causes of a patient's heart failure are both key to positive long term outcome and prognosis. HF medical treatments include:

- Oxygen protocol
- Diagnostic tests – Such as blood urea nitrogen, serum creatinine, sodium, chloride, potassium, and magnesium levels
- Daily weights and monitoring of fluid intake and output (I & O)
- Assessment of vitals
- Skin care
- Consultation with dietician
- Low sodium, low fluid diet.
- Drug therapy (discussed later)
- Encourage rest
- Anxiety and stress relief
- Upright positioning to promote oxygenation via maximum chest expansion (semi-Fowler's or high Fowler's position)

- Monitor for complications (pulmonary edema, dysrhythmias, and hypokalemia)
- Patient teaching such as dietary restrictions, daily weighing, and reporting of any recurring symptoms, such as SOB, cough, weight gain, loss of appetite, leg edema, and frequent night urination

Coronary Artery Disease (CAD)

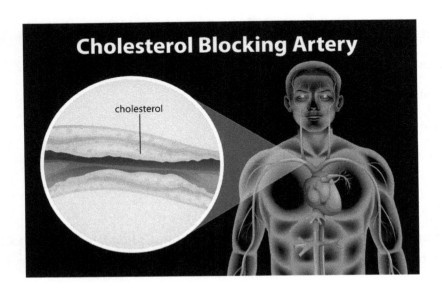

Coronary artery disease (CAD) is considered to be the largest single killer of Americans (both male and female) within any cultural group. One American dies every 33 seconds from this cardiac disease. CAD results from interactions of the following conditions:

- Atherosclerotic Plaque – Narrowing and/or hardening of arteries from an excessive buildup of fatty, fibrous plaque which can eventually rupture
- Aggregation of platelets
- Formation of thrombi (clots)
- Vasoconstriction – Narrowing of a blood vessel as a result of contraction of its muscular wall)

Contributing Factors of CAD

- Accumulation of lipoproteins in the vessels
- Chronic inflammation of the vessels

Problems of CAD

Two major problems occur in coronary artery disease. These include:

- Ischemia – Occurs when insufficient oxygen is supplied to meet requirements of the myocardium
- Infarction – Occurs when ischemia is severe and prolonged – results in irreversible cardiac tissue damage

Risk Factors for CAD

- Elevated levels of LDL cholesterol (> 130mg/dl) and triglycerides (> 200mg/dl)
- Hypertension
- Obesity
- Diabetes
- Being male until > 75 years of age, then there is equal risk
- Smoking

Diagnostic Evaluation of CAD

- Fasting triglycerides
- Serum cholesterol panel (total cholesterol, LDL, HDL, VLDL, LDL:HDL ratio)
- Cardiac C-reactive protein (CRP) blood test

Acute Coronary Syndrome (ACS)

Acute coronary syndrome (ACS) is an "umbrella term" used to describe situations where the heart muscle's blood supply is blocked suddenly. It includes two cardiac "emergency" conditions.

These include:

- Unstable angina
- Myocardial infarction (MI)

Angina

Also known as "angina pectoris," angina is a Latin term meaning either "pain of the chest" or "strangling of the chest." Angina is not a disease *per se*, but a symptom of ischemia caused by insufficient blood flow to the myocardium. Angina occurs when the demand for oxygen exceeds the supply, and thus, the heart is not receiving enough oxygen. Since the heart itself does not have nerves, which are sensitive, pain is felt elsewhere, causing "referred pain." The affected coronary artery may be 75% occluded before a patient experiences any pain.

Symptoms of Angina

An angina "attack" typically lasts less than 10 or 15 minutes. Symptoms can include:

- Substernal pain
- Heaviness of the chest
- Tightness of the chest
- Pressure of the chest
- Squeezing of the chest
- Burning of the chest
- Pain radiating to the arm(s), neck, jaw, shoulders, and/or throat (described as "choking" or "strangling")
- Shortness of breath (SOB)
- Nausea/vomiting
- Diaphoresis (excessive sweating)
- Anxiety
- Apprehension

Commonly, angina symptoms will be relieved by:

- Rest

- Oxygen

- Nitroglycerine (decreases demand and increases oxygen supply)

- Removing the precipitating cause(s)

Angina Risk Factors (Triggers)

- Exercise or exertion

- Stress or emotions

- Cold

- Overeating

- High altitudes

Diagnostic Evaluation of Angina

- Clinical pain manifestations

- Detailed patient history

- ECG (and ECG changes)

- Tests – Includes stress test, chest x-ray, cardiac catheterization, coronary angiography, computed tomography, angiography, as well as blood cholesterol, sugar, and protein levels

Objectives of Medical Management of Angina

- Decreasing the myocardium's demand for oxygen.

- Increasing oxygen supply to the myocardium.

Types of Angina

- "Stable" angina – Occurs on exertion and symptoms stay stable for several months. Typically, there is only slight activity limitation and stable angina is manageable with medications.

- "Unstable" angina – An unpredictable, transient episode of prolonged, severe discomfort which appears at rest. The patient has either never experienced this feeling before or it is much worse than during previous episodes. Symptoms mimic a myocardial infarction (MI).

> **NOTE: UNSTABLE ANGINA IS A RED FLAG SIGN OF POTENTIAL MYOCARDIAL INFARCTION **

Angina Treatment, Prevention, and Education

<u>Treatment</u>

- Nitroglycerine – If ordered, patient should always carry the pills and place under the tongue as required. The typical dosage is up to 3 tabs administered 5 minutes apart

- Rest – Stop and rest until pain goes away, as patient should get relief in 1-3 minutes

- Call doctor and go to ER, if necessary

<u>Prevention</u>

- Alternate periods of activity and rest
- Control diet
- Avoid cold temperatures
- Avoid smoking, caffeine, and over-the-counter medications

<u>Education</u>

- Only take meds as prescribed.
- Awareness of drug side effects

Myocardial Infarction (MI)

More commonly known as a "heart attack," a myocardial infarction occurs when myocardial tissue is destroyed (death and necrosis) in heart regions that have been deprived of an adequate blood supply. MI is caused by either:

- Narrowing of a coronary artery or arteries as a result of atherosclerosis
- Complete occlusion (blockage of an artery due to an embolus or thrombus)

Characteristics/Duration of MI Pain

- Persistent, severe substernal pain or pain over the pericardium
- May radiate widely throughout the chest
- May be accompanied by pain in the shoulders, jaw, neck, teeth, hands, and/or arms (especially left arm)
- Described as "viselike," "squeezing," and/or "crushing"
- Typically lasts longer than 15 minutes and can last as long as 12 hours
- Occurs spontaneously or may follow an attack of unstable angina
- Not necessarily, but may be related to stress, exercise, and/or exertion.
- Not relieved by rest, nitroglycerine, and/or oxygen
- Increasing in severity until almost unbearable

Associated Signs and Symptoms of MI

- Fatigue
- Feeling of impending doom
- SOB
- Nausea and vomiting
- Anxiety
- Coolness of the extremities
- Perspiring
- Hypotension or hypertension

- Arrhythmias
- Muffled heart sounds
- Palpable precordial pulse

MI Risk Factors

- Male
- Age over 40 years
- Previous history of atherosclerosis
- Hypertension
- Smoking
- Birth control pill use

MI in Women

Heart attacks are also big killers of women, with 40% of cases being fatal as women do not always recognize the symptoms. Signs and symptoms can manifest differently in women. Symptoms include:

- Feeling breathless
- Often do not experience chest pain of any kind
- Flu-like symptoms such as nausea, cold sweats, and/or clamminess
- Fatigue, weakness, and/or dizziness that is not explained
- Anxiety
- Abdominal, upper back, shoulder, and/or jaw pain

Diagnostic Evaluation of MI

- ECG findings (may be normal or inconclusive)
- Echocardiography
- Creatine kinase (CK) elevated
- White blood cells (WBC) elevated

Objectives of Medical/Nursing Management of MI

- The main goal of management is to minimize damage to the myocardium, as much as possible with immediate assessment

- Relieve chest pain

- Provide rest

- Prevent of complications

Medical Interventions and Nursing Treatments for MI

The prognosis of MI depends on three main factors: severity of the obstruction of the coronary artery, extent of damage to the myocardium, and how rapidly the patient receives treatment. In an ideal situation, the patient should have an ECG within 10 minutes of arriving at the emergency room door. For the patient who has an MI, emergency treatments initiated by a cardiac/vascular nurse include:

- Elevating head of bed/stretcher

- Oxygen administration

Medical orders may also include:

- Morphine sulfate to decrease patient's anxiety level and workload on the heart muscle

- Intravenous line for heparin, fluids, etc.

- Stat cardiac profile and ECG

- ASA, Plavix, and/or nitrates

- Stool softeners to reduce straining during bowel movements

- Immediate angiogram and stent placement

- Transfer to ICU

- Monitor closely for first 48 hours including vitals and I&O

- Reduced activity to lessen heart's demand for oxygen – This involves complete bed rest, including bedside commode, for first 24 to 48 hours then gradually increase level of activity including bathroom privileges

Peripheral Artery Disease (PAD)

Peripheral artery disease (PAD) is defined as gradual occlusion (blockage) of the aorta and its major arterial branches, which leads to hypoxia (oxygen deprivation) and necrosis of affected tissues. PAD is a common complication of atherosclerosis, which results in loss of elasticity as well as calcification of the walls of the arteries. This can cause an interruption of blood flow, typically to the legs and/or feet. An occlusion can develop quickly or very slowly over the course of 20 to 40 years. The prognosis depends on occlusion location, development of collateral circulation to make up for decreased blood flow, as well as the time between development and removal of blockage. In advanced cases of peripheral artery disease, necrosis, ulceration, and/or gangrene can result.

Five P's of Acute Occlusion

> **P -** Pain or Intermittent Claudication – This pain results in discomfort or cramping within lower extremity muscles, which is caused by obstruction of the arteries or deep veins and occurs on exertion
>
> **P -** Pallor – Lightening or color changes in an extremity
>
> **P -** Pulselessness – This is the absence of pulses in the affected extremity
>
> **P -** Paresthesia – Involves tingling and/or prickling sensations caused by pressure or damage to the peripheral nerves
>
> **P -** Paralysis – This results from pressure or damage to the peripheral nerves

Risk Factors for Peripheral Artery Disease

- Aging
- Hypertension
- Smoking
- Diabetes
- Myocardial infarction
- Stroke
- Family history of vascular disorders
- Hyperlipidemia (high serum lipid levels)
- Male gender

Diagnostic Evaluation of PAD

- Arteriography
- Ultrasonography
- Doppler
- Pulse volume measurements
- Computer tomography (CT scan)

Medical/Surgical Interventions for PAD

- Decrease risks of cardiovascular disease (control diabetes and hypertension)
- Stop smoking
- Prevent any further trauma and skin breakdown of the affected extremity, such as use of footboard, foot cradle, and heel protectors to relieve pressure)
- Medications, such as anti-platelet therapy (ASA), ACE inhibitors, and thrombolytics
- Analgesics to relieve pain
- Surgical procedures, such as embolectomy, endarterectomy, arterial bypass, balloon angioplasty, percutaneous transluminal coronary angioplasty (PCTA)

Age-Related Changes

While there are many lifestyle choices an individual can consciously make to decrease the risks of developing cardiac/vascular diseases, there are certain normal physiological changes that take place within the heart and its associated vessels as a person ages. Changes associated with normal aging include:

- Calcification of the cardiac valves
- Conduction time increases
- The left ventricle of the heart increases in size
- The aorta and other large arteries of the heart thicken and become stiffer

- Baroreceptors are nerve cells located within the carotid arteries and aortic arch that respond to pressure changes within the blood vessels and influence heart rate. With age, these cells become less sensitive

Probing Questions About Cardiac/Vascular History

In addition to the cardiovascular patient's health history questions mentioned above, a cardiac/vascular nurse should develop the necessary skills to ask other probing cardiovascular-related health history questions. Inquire about the following signs and symptoms:

- Shortness of breath when resting, at night and/or upon exertion
- Cough
- Pallor and/or cyanosis
- Fatigue
- Weakness
- Dizziness
- Headaches
- Hypertension or hypotension
- Unexplained changes in weight, either loss or gain
- Any peripheral skin changes including color, reduced distribution of hair, and a shiny, thin appearance

Performing Systematic Physical Assessments Using the Appropriate Tools

The cardiac/vascular nurse should develop the skills necessary to perform various systemic assessments of cardiovascular patients utilizing the appropriate tools. For example, they should be able to administer procedures using a Doppler ultrasound device, pulse oximeter, as well as a telemetry monitor. A cardiac/vascular nurse also needs to be able to interpret the assessment findings and associated test results in order to accurately report them to the patient's cardiovascular specialist or other medical professionals involved in a CV patient's care and treatment plan.

Doppler Ultrasound

A Doppler ultrasound device is a non-invasive method used to measure the flow of blood within veins and arteries. A Doppler aids in the assessment of vascular conditions such as intermittent claudication, aneurysms, and PAD. This diagnostic is utilized to measure the ankle-brachial index (ABI). ABI is defined as the ratio of blood pressure within the lower legs to blood pressure within the arms. If the leg blood pressure is lower than that in the arm, this is an indication of occluded arteries. In order to perform an ABI test on a cardiac/vascular patient, the CV nurse should perform the following steps:

1. Clearly explain the purpose of the procedure as well as the steps involved in performing the test.

2. Gather the necessary equipment.

3. Thoroughly wash the hands.

4. Apply warm conductive jelly to the patient's arm, in the spot where the brachial pulse is felt.

5. Obtain and then record this systolic pressure reading. Repeat on the other arm.

6. Find the posterior tibial pulse (on the medial aspect of the ankle) and repeat step #5 on both legs.

7. Locate the dorsalis pedal pulse (on the dorsal aspect of the foot) and repeat step #5 on both legs.

8. Take these readings and calculate the ABI. Use the following formula:

9. Divide the higher of the two systolic pressures (either the dorsalis pedis or the posterior tibial) by the higher of the two brachial systolic blood pressures. Example: Left posterior tibial systolic pressure = 128, left dorsalis pedis systolic pressure = 130, left brachial systolic pressure = 132. ABI = 130/132 or 0.98.

Interpreting ABI Results

- ABI > 1.30 = Non-compressible arteries considered abnormal (often seen in patients who have diabetes and/or renal failure as well as in heavy smokers)

- ABI –1.0 to 1.29 = Normal

- ABI – 0.91 to 0.99 = Borderline PAD

- ABI – 0.41 to 0.90 = Mild to moderate PAD

- ABI – .00 to 0.40 = Severe PAD

Pulse Oximetry

Pulse oximetry monitoring is a simple, non-invasive procedure than may be performed either intermittently or continuously in order to monitor a CV patient's arterial oxygen saturation. A baseline reading should also be taken on admission for all patients. Hypoxemia (low blood oxygen) indicates that there is a lower than normal level of oxygen in the blood. The body requires a certain blood oxygen level in order to nourish its cells and tissues so that they can function properly. When this level of oxygen falls below a certain percentage, hypoxemia occurs and a patient can experience dyspnea.

Pulse oximetry monitoring may be performed to assess if a patient has adequate blood oxygen levels in a variety of medical conditions including heart failure (HF), myocardial infarction (MI), chronic obstructive pulmonary disease (COPD), and anemia. Two light emitting diodes (LEDs) send infrared and red light through a pulsating arterial vascular bed. This is typically accomplished by clipping a small pulse oximeter device onto one of the patient's fingertips or earlobes. A photo-detector measures the transmitted light while it passes through the vascular bed. Measuring the amount of color absorbed by the arterial blood, it calculates the precise arterial oxygen saturation.

Arterial oxygen saturation is indicated by the symbol SpO2. While pulse oximetry actually measures blood oxygen saturation, results are often used to estimate blood oxygen levels. Under the majority of circumstances, normal pulse oximetry readings range from 95 to 100 percent. Pulse oximeter readings of less than 90 percent are considered to be low and indicative of hypoxia.

Telemetry Monitoring

When a CV patient is admitted to hospital, one of the first procedures that should be performed is continuous cardiac monitoring. Continuous observation of the electrical activity of the heart is used in specific cardiovascular disorders where a patient is at an increased risk for arrhythmias that can prove to be life-threatening. Similar to other forms of electrocardiography, cardiac monitoring 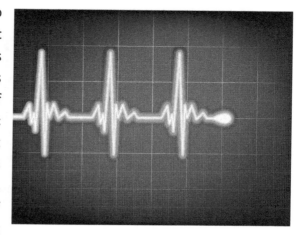 utilizes electrodes that are placed on the chest of the patient in order to transmit electrical signals. These signals are then converted into a cardiac rhythm tracing on an oscilloscope, which is a scope that measures both the voltage and frequency of an electric signal using a visual display.

There are two different types of monitoring that can be performed: hardwire or telemetry). In the case of hardwire monitoring, the patient is directly hooked up to a bedside monitor. A heart rhythm display will appear continuously at both the bedside and the remote console. On the other hand, telemetry utilizes a small transmitter which is connected to the chest of an ambulatory patient by way of electrodes. This portable device transmits the heart's electrical signals to another location where they are displayed on a monitoring screen. Regardless of the kind of cardiac monitor, it accurately displays a CV patient's heart rate and rhythm as well as recognizing and counting any abnormal heart beats. An alarm will go off if the heart rate goes higher or lower than previously specified limits.

Conditions Requiring Telemetry

- Previous history of heart disease
- Angina pectoris
- Arrhythmias
- Changes in heart medications
- Electrolyte abnormalities
- Unexplained syncope

Nursing Considerations Related to Telemetry

- Ensure that all electrical equipment and outlets are properly grounded to avoid the potential for electrical shock and/or interference. In addition, make sure that the patient is clean and dry to prevent electrical shock

- If the patient's skin is particularly scaly, oily, or sweaty, rub the sites where the electrodes will be positioned with dry 4" by 4" gauze pads before application of the electrodes in order to assist in the reduction of interference in the tracings

- Every 24 hours, assess the integrity of the patient's skin. If required, reposition the electrodes

- At least every 8 hours, document a rhythm strip, along with any changes in the patient's condition, or as stated by the policies of the medical facility

Interpreting Telemetry Results

- Manual Method: Remove a rhythm strip from the machine. The heart rhythm is printed on grid paper. Typically, it measures time by utilizing a scale of 25 millimeters which represents 1 second. In addition, there will be other marks, referred to as hash marks, located at the top or bottom of the telemetry strip. They represent intervals of 1 second or 3 seconds.

- Six Seconds Times Ten Method: The six second count method is the most common and simplest method to determine a patient's heart rate. Take the total number of QRS complexes detected over a period of six seconds and multiply by a factor 10. This provides the number of QRS complexes in 1 minute (patient's heart rate). Example: 8 QRS complexes within 6 seconds x 10 = HR of 80.

- Triplicate Method: The triplicate method can only be used with a regular heart rhythm. Each large square of the telemetry strip equals 5 millimeters (1/5 of a second). Find an R wave (spikes in the readout) that fall on a thick vertical line. Then, locate the next R wave and the R wave following that. Begin with a heart rate of 300. Divide 300 by the total number of large telemetry squares found between the R waves. If each R wave occurs with just one large square in between them, the heart rate will be 300. However, if there are 4 large squares in between R waves, the heart rate is 75 beats per minute.

- Caliper Method: This particular method is the most accurate calculation. It counts the total number of millimeters between R to R intervals by using a pair of calipers. A one-minute telemetry strip has a total of 1,500 millimeters (25 millimeters/second x 60). Divide 1500 by the total millimeters found in the R to R interval. The result is the patient's heart rate. Example, if there are 20 millimeters locate within the R to R interval, then 1500/20 = HR of 75

Obtaining Pertinent Data from Multiple Sources

The cardiac/vascular nurse should develop the skills necessary to obtain pertinent data from multiple sources besides the patient. This includes laboratory values, invasive and noninvasive test results, and medical consultations. For example, a cardiovascular patient will have an ongoing history of medical assessments and treatments from their primary care provider, including laboratory test results and findings from previous procedures. In addition, the patient will likely have letters of consultation from the family physician as well as cardiac/vascular and other medical/surgical specialists.

A CV nurse should possess the appropriate investigative skills to obtain and subsequently extract any relevant information associated with the patient's chief cardiovascular complaint. This is needed in order to obtain a thorough cardiovascular assessment and possible treatments.

Blood Tests Used to Assess/Diagnose Myocardial Infarction

Following an MI, damaged cardiac tissues release significant quantities of proteins and enzymes into the bloodstream. Specific blood tests assist in the confirmation of an MI diagnosis, show the degree of heart damage, help in monitoring the healing process, and assess reperfusion (restoration of blood flow to the heart) following administration of fibrinolytics (thrombolytic drugs used to dissolve blood clots). These laboratory tests include:

- Serum cardiac biomarkers such as myoglobin, creatine kinase (CK), and CK-MB
- Troponin I
- Troponin T

Blood Tests Used to Evaluate Heart Disease Risk

- Homocysteine (tHcy)

- High-sensitivity C-reactive protein (hs-CRP)

- Triglycerides

- Total cholesterol

- HDL, LDL, VLDL

Blood Tests Used to Evaluate Heart Failure Risk

- A-type natriuretic peptide (ANP)

- B-type natriuretic peptide (BNP)

Blood Tests Used to Evaluate Overall Health and Treatment Responses

- Electrolytes, such as potassium, calcium, magnesium, sodium chloride, and carbon dioxide

- Coagulation tests including activated clotting time (ACT), partial thromboplastin time (PTT), prothrombin time with INR (PT w/INR)

Non-Invasive Test Results

- Electrocardiogram (ECG) – See description above under telemetry monitoring

- Echocardiogram – This involves ultra-high frequency sound waves which examine size, shape, and motion of cardiac structures

- Doppler – See description above under Doppler ultrasound

- Stress Test – Includes ECG, treadmill, and exercise

- Holter Monitoring – This is an ambulatory ECG

- Magnetic Resonance Imaging (MRI) – This gives 3D cardiac images

- Positron Emission Tomography (PET) – This provides heart images

- Cardiac Blood Pool Imaging – This evaluates regional and global ventricular performance

Invasive Test Results

- Cardiac Catheterization – With this procedure, a catheter is passed through veins and arteries in order to perform various cardiac tests (heart/artery pressures, blood flow, valve competence, etc.)

- Transesophageal Electrocardiography – This is an ultrasound combined with endoscopy to better visualize heart structures

- Chest Radiography – This test uses ionizing radiation

- Venography – This is a radiographic examination of lower extremity veins using contrast medium

- Peripheral Angiography – This is a radiographic examination of peripheral arteries and veins using contrast medium

Identifying Missing Information

After obtaining a complete patient history, performing a thorough physical examination, gathering pertinent diagnostic test results and clinical findings supplied by other medical professionals, the cardiac/vascular nurse needs the appropriate skills to synthesize all this information. As part of this process, they must identify if there is any information missing from the patient's overall assessment. If there is potentially valuable information missing, the CV nurse needs to either locate it and/or inform the CV specialist(s) so they can order additional tests and/or procedures.

A CV nurse must have the skills to interpret all the assessment findings and pertinent test results. They must prioritize a patient's individual assessment findings and tests results in order to compare them to standardized normal ranges. This information is combined with the patient's key historical indicators, such as previous cardiovascular events, associated treatments, and/or surgical procedures. This is necessary for the healthcare provider to formulate an accurate, appropriate nursing diagnosis.

The Nursing Diagnosis

In order to formulate an accurate and appropriate nursing diagnosis for a specific CV patient, the nurse must have the necessary knowledge to identify nursing diagnoses related to cardiac/vascular conditions. They must also possess the skills to both formulate and prioritize individualized nursing diagnoses.

According to NANDA International, a nursing diagnosis is defined as "a clinical judgment about actual or potential individual, family, or community responses to health problems/life processes." A nursing diagnosis also "provides the basis for selection of nursing interventions to achieve outcomes for which the nurse has accountability."

Types of Nursing Diagnosis

In generalized medical nursing terms, there are actually four types of nursing diagnoses. These categories can be extrapolated to the cardiac/vascular patient/nursing care setting as well.

1. *Actual Nursing Diagnosis* – An actual nursing diagnosis is a clinical nursing judgment concerning the patient's actual experiences and responses to various normal life processes or health conditions.

2. *Health-Promotion Nursing Diagnosis* – The health-promotion nursing diagnosis is a clinical judgment regarding a patient's, their family's health and well-being, and the community's desire or motivation to increase well-being and health potential. The desire/motivation is expressed by their readiness to embrace specific health behaviors.

3. *Risk Nursing Diagnosis* – A risk nursing diagnosis describes vulnerable patients' responses to various normal life processes and health conditions. It is supported by the presence of known risk factors.

4. *Syndrome Nursing Diagnosis* – A syndrome nursing diagnosis is a clinical judgment that describes specific clusters of nursing diagnoses that happen together. They tend to be addressed as a group and by implementing similar interventions (NANDA International, 2014).

Prioritizing Nursing Diagnoses

The following is a list of steps that any nurse, including a CV nurse, can use to systematically prioritize their nursing diagnoses. Some of these steps have been described in more detail earlier on in this document.

1. Review the patient's pre-admission diagnosis by using appropriate nursing textbooks and/or other scientific reference materials.

2. Review the patient's chart for any co-morbidities (i.e. at least two co-existing medical conditions or diseases) in illness history, previous hospitalizations, and surgeries.

3. Research the possible nursing diagnoses and/or any collaborative problems by using current editions of appropriate medical/surgical nursing texts and/or other scientific reference materials. These will tend to be the highest priority nursing diagnoses.

4. Make potential diagnoses using the PES format: Problem, Etiology, and Signs/Symptoms. Do this for every nursing diagnosis and/or collaborative problem.

5. Examine the patient's medication profile prior to hospital admission. Ensure the patient continues to receive these medication(s) while in hospital or make sure there is a logical reason why they have been discontinued.

6. Make sure the patient's past medical history lined up with the medical disorders that he or she had medications prescribed for pre-admission to hospital.

7. Make nursing diagnoses for every diagnosis and collaborative problem and/or add them to a data cluster for prior identified diagnoses.

8. Examine every health pattern in the assessment database. Make nursing diagnoses for every normal deviation where a data cluster exists supporting its use.

9. Review all laboratory values and diagnostic results. Identify any noticeable gaps in this information.

10. Review the patient's current hospital medication profile. Refer to a current drug guide regarding collaborative care and add it to a data cluster for a diagnosis that has already been developed. Make nursing diagnoses for every diagnosis and/or collaborative problem as was done for pre-admission medications.

11. Review all nursing notes for the individual patient. This process will shed light on the context of the patient's current experiences while care is being given. Start to list nursing diagnoses and/or collaborative problems.

All patient care diagnoses are not necessarily listed within a nursing care plan book. Hence, refer to appropriate medical/surgical textbooks for collaborative care. After completing the above steps, number the diagnoses and collaborative problems in order of priority.

Planning and Implementation (22%)

Effective planning and implementation, within the cardiac/vascular clinical setting, involves having the necessary knowledge and skills to plan and implement an individualized patient care plan as well as knowledge of pharmacological considerations related to the cardiac/vascular patient.

The Individualized Plan of Care

In order to effectively plan and implement an individualized plan of care, a CV nurse must have sufficient knowledge of various evidence-based treatment options for the cardiac/vascular patient, as well as certain complementary therapies. In addition, the cardiac/vascular nurse must possess skills in the following areas:

- Developing the individualized cardiac/vascular patient's plan of care by involving their family members, significant others, caregivers, and other members of the interdisciplinary team

- Performing interventions according to the evidence-based practice guidelines

- Coordinating patient care with the interdisciplinary team

- Using clinical judgment, such as responding to acute changes, critical thinking, and problem solving

- Formulating outcomes

Evidence-Based Treatment

Evidence-based medicine necessitates what is known as a "bottom-up approach." This approach takes the best external evidence and combines it with the individual expertise of the clinician and the choice of the patient. Integrating these three components allows the physician and patient to enhance clinical decisions. Thus, opportunities for optimum quality of life and the best clinical outcomes for the patient can be realized.

Quality Cardiovascular Measures

In 2012, the National Quality Forum (NQF) approved 39 quality cardiovascular measures. These measures address a vast range of cardiovascular diseases and disorders as well as associated procedures, diagnostic studies, treatments, and interventions. These cardiovascular conditions include:

- Hypertension

- Heart failure

- Acute myocardial infarction

- Coronary artery disease

- Percutaneous coronary intervention

- Atrial fibrillation

The mission of NQF is to improve the overall quality of healthcare in America by way of the following three measures:

- Achieving consensus on national goals and priorities for improvement in performance as well as working in partnership in order to reach these priorities/goals

- Endorsing standards of national consensus for measurements and public performance reports

- Promoting attainment of national goals via outreach and education programs

The NQF database of 39 quality measures related to care is available at: http://www.qualityforum.org/News_And_Resources/Press_Releases/2012/NQF_Endors es_Cardiovascular_Measures.aspx (National Quality Forum, 2010).

CHEST Guidelines

Based on rigorous methodology, CHEST guidelines strive to meet the highest guideline standards as outlined by the Institute of Medicine. The CHEST guidelines are utilized all over the world and across many different medical specialties. With respect to the cardiac/vascular patient, the core guidelines concern both the prevention and treatment of thrombosis.

This represents significant effort to make possible the translation of quality evidence into relevant interventions within the clinical setting in order to improve both patient-focused care and outcomes. It is important to note that medical education, nursing care, quality of care, and healthcare policy can have a science based foundation rather than just a beliefs base.

You can find the CHEST Guidelines online at http://journal.publications.chestnet.org/ss/guidelines.aspx

Within these guidelines are more than 600 recommendations including the diagnosis, treatment and prevention of thrombosis as well as a comprehensive list that addresses clinical conditions such as stroke, cardiovascular disease, and atrial fibrillation.

AHA/ACC Guidelines for the Cardiac/Vascular Patient

Cardiac/vascular disease prevention guidelines were recently written by the American Heart Association (AHA) and the American College of Cardiology (ACC). These guidelines were released in November, 2013. Based on many years of scientific research, these CVD guidelines were written in order to develop the best approaches in the prevention of stroke and heart disease, considered the leading causes of death worldwide.

A risk assessment performed by either a healthcare provider or cardiac/vascular nurse should be based on certain personalized risk factors. These include:

- Race
- Age
- Gender
- Heart
- Hypertension
- Stroke

Risk Calculators

Risk calculators are utilized in order to assess a patient's personal risk which sets the stage for discussions with their healthcare provider and other medical professionals.

- Race: There are increased degrees of CVD risk in the African-American population, and according to the patient's personal stroke risks.

- Obesity: Treatments for obesity are done using a team based approach. Also, strategies for effective weight loss are based on body mass index (BMI). Healthy diet combined with exercise still works best.

- Cholesterol: Overall health status and cholesterol risks factors are what guide a patient's treatment plan. A CV patient's "bad cholesterol" levels are no longer the chief factor guiding their plan of care. Drug treatment decisions are based on collaborative discussions with the patient's healthcare provider

- Lifestyle: Encourage 40 minutes of exercise to be done 3 to 4 times weekly. Also, advise the patient on a diet rich in fruit and vegetables and a reduced sodium intake

Vascular Disease Foundation Guidelines

Peripheral arterial disease (PAD) refers to occlusive, stenotic, and aneurysmal diseases of the aorta and its branch arteries (specifically the coronary arteries). The following practice guidelines have been developed to help clinical physicians in making appropriate decisions by describing the generally accepted diagnostic and/or management approaches for PAD patients.

The scope of these guidelines includes abdominal aortic, renal, mesenteric, and lower extremity arterial disorders. It is important to realize that PAD patients tend to possess co-existing cardiac and/or cerebrovascular conditions. Thus, they have an increased risk of myocardial infarction and ischemic events and an increased risk of mortality from coronary heart disease and/or stroke. Attention to the overall cardiovascular system and reduction of risk factors is particularly important.

These guidelines try to define clinical practices that meet the majority of patients' needs, in the majority of circumstances. Obviously, ultimate judgments concerning individual care must be made by the physician in collaboration with the patient taking all their personal circumstances into consideration. Also, these recommendations are tailored specifically to the PAD patient's primary care physician, internist, cardiac/vascular nurse and nurse practitioner, as well as cardiac and vascular specialists and their trainees.

Classification of Recommendations

- Class I - Conditions where there is evidence and/or general agreement that given procedure(s) and/or treatment(s) are beneficial, useful as well as effective.

- Class II - Any conditions where there is either conflicting evidence or divergence of opinions concerning the usefulness and efficacy of treatment(s) or procedure(s).

- Class IIa - Weight of evidence/opinion is in favor of usefulness/efficacy.

- Class IIb - Usefulness and/or effectiveness are not as well established by either evidence or opinions.

- Class III - Conditions where the evidence and/or general agreement is that treatments and/or procedures will not be useful and/or effective. In some cases, they may prove to be harmful to the patient.

Levels of Evidence

A. Data obtained from multiple evidence-based randomized clinical trials and/or meta-analyses.

B. Data derived from either a single randomized control trial or non-randomized studies.

C. There is only expert consensus of opinion, case studies and/or existing standards of care.

Full Text Guidelines and a Pocket PDF Guide can be found at:

http://vasculardisease.org/for-professionals/additional-professional-resources/medical-guidelines/

Complementary Therapies

In addition to gaining pertinent knowledge concerning evidence-based treatment options, a cardiac/vascular nurse should also have adequate knowledge of complementary "alternative" therapies, including relaxation and acupuncture.

Relaxation Techniques

Relaxation techniques include many different practices, such as guided imagery, progressive relaxation, biofeedback, self-hypnosis, and deep breathing exercises. All have similar goals, which are to consciously promote the natural relaxation responses of the body. In fact, relaxation is more than a state of mind. Rather, it physically changes the way the body functions. Natural relaxation responses are characterized by:

- A slower respiratory rate
- Lower blood pressure
- Decreased oxygen consumption
- Overall feelings of calmness and/or well-being

Individuals often utilize relaxation techniques as part of an overall treatment plan in order to effectively:

- Release "pent-up" tension
- Counteract negative effects of stress
- Reduce anxiety and depression
- Calm emotions
- Promote sleep
- Reduce headaches
- Decrease pain levels

Other noteworthy facts about relaxation techniques include:

- Generally considered to be safe.
- Should not be used as a replacement for evidence-based treatments or to delay consulting a doctor about an ongoing medical issue.
- All health care providers should be informed about any complementary healthcare approaches a patient uses. Doing so will assist in the coordination of a safe plan of care.
- Relaxation techniques are most beneficial when practiced on a regular basis as well as when used in combination with other forms of regular exercise, a healthy diet and a strong support system of relatives and/or friends.

Acupuncture

Acupuncture, an ancient Chinese "holistic" medical approach, is based on treating all of the systems of the body. Some of the benefits of acupuncture include improvement of physical health conditions or disorders, as well as instilling feelings of increased mental clarity. This ancient Chinese medical technique works directly with the body's energy, also known as the "qi." Practitioners of acupuncture believe that illnesses are caused by weakness and depletion of the natural "energy flow" throughout the body thus making a patient more susceptible to illnesses.

Acupuncture "rebalances" the body's energy by way of inserting sterile, disposable needles into specific "acupoints." These points are related to the chief symptoms or illness of the patient. Treatments are thought to effectively remove any obstructions to the flow of bodily energy. Various clinical trials have proven that acupuncture is effective in treating many medical conditions. Thus, its use has been incorporated into conventional Western medical practices. Acupuncture treatments can result in faster recovery times from acute injuries, reduced stress symptoms, and improved circulation in the cardiovascular patient.

While acupuncture is most effective as a method of pain control, it also benefits other health conditions related to the CV patient. These include possible relief of:

- Paralysis following a stroke
- Improved peripheral and/or systemic circulation
- Anxiety
- Depression
- Stress

Acupuncture can effectively eliminate, or at least decrease, ongoing requirements for pain medications or drugs which are administered to relieve symptoms of various health conditions. In addition, acupuncture is often utilized as a method of preventative medicine. Many people receive acupuncture treatments without actually suffering from any particular illness or disease since it can strengthen an individual's overall immune system, which results in a generalized state of well-being.

Developing the Individualized Care Plan

It is the cardiac/vascular nurse's responsibility to develop a patient's individualized care plan and ensure that all components are included and updated as necessary. The care plan provides direction for individualized care, based on the patient's own list of diagnoses and organized according to specific needs. It also provides continuity of care. The plan is a communication/organization method of actions for a constantly changing nursing staff. As the patient's needs are met, the plan is updated and passed on to the next shift during nursing rounds.

The care plan clearly spells out observations to make, nursing interventions to carry out and instructions that the patient/family need. It also is a guide for staffing for patient care. Care may need to be assigned to nursing staff with particular skills. Additionally, an individualized care plan is a guide for reimbursement, utilized by insurance companies to decide what they will pay for. Nursing care must be documented precisely. Otherwise, there is no proof care was given and insurers will not pay.

Format of Care Plans

Exact formatting of nursing care plans varies slightly from facility to facility. Generally, they are organized by four categories. These include:

- Nursing diagnoses (problem list): Defines appropriate patient care plan and drives interventions and patient outcomes.

- Goals and outcomes: These are observable client responses and desired change(s) in patient's condition.

- Nursing orders: Specific instructions for nursing activities that will be performed to assist the patient in achieving health care goal(s).

- Evaluation: The healthcare team can determine patient's progress towards achievement of goals and the nursing care plan's effectiveness. This is very important as evaluating the plan determines whether nursing interventions need to be continued, changed or terminated.

Performing Interventions According to Evidence-Based Practice Guidelines

A nursing intervention is defined as "any act by a nurse that implements the nursing care plan or any specific objective of that plan." A patient may require intervention in the form of limitation, support, medication, and treatment for the current condition. Intervention might also be needed to prevent any further stress from developing. As stress increases, the need to adapt increases as does the need for appropriate nursing intervention(s).

The cardiac/vascular nurse should perform required nursing interventions according to the various evidence-based practice guidelines as discussed above. Examples of cardiac/vascular nursing interventions include:

- Promoting rest or activity (at appropriate times).

- Frequent turning and/or proper positioning.

- Promoting relief from anxiety and/or stress.

- Providing skin care, as necessary.

- Monitoring bowel movements and administering stool softeners, as required.

- Measuring input and output.

- Recording vital signs and reporting any major changes to the doctor.

- Watching for complications, such as edema, abnormal heart sounds, pallor, cyanosis, SOB, and cough

- Monitoring of blood test results, such as for hypokalemia, hyperkalemia, hyponatremia, etc.

- Performing diagnostic tests

- Following O2 protocol

- Arranging consultations with other members of the interdisciplinary team (e.g. cardiologist, dietician, social worker, psychologist, physical therapist, pharmacist, and spiritual leader

- Offering appropriate diet

- Administering ordered medications

Coordinating Care with the Interdisciplinary Team

An interdisciplinary team is made up of various practitioners from different professions. Within a particular medical facility or healthcare network, they all share a common patient population as well as common patient care goals, and have responsibility for complementary tasks. In addition, the patient and their support system, such as immediate family members, significant others, and caregivers, all are essential members of the team and must be consulted when formulating realistic treatment plan goals and health care outcomes.

The team works interdependently and establishes ongoing communication amongst team members, patients and their support system to ensure that all aspects of a patient's health care needs are integrated and properly addressed. Another of the cardiac/vascular nurse's responsibilities is to ensure that a CV patient's care is well coordinated using the interdisciplinary team.

Benefits of Interdisciplinary Team Care	
For the Patient • Improves care by increasing coordination of services, especially for complex problems • Integrates health care for a vast range of needs and/or problems • Empowers patients as active care partners • May serve patients of diverse cultural backgrounds • More efficient time use	**For Healthcare Professionals** • Increases levels of professional satisfaction • Facilitates a shift from acute, episodic care to emphasis on long-term preventive care • Enables the practitioner to learn new approaches and/or skills • Promotes innovation • Allows health care providers to focus on their individualized areas of expertise
For Educators and Students • Provides multiple health care approaches for study • Fosters understanding and appreciation of other disciplines • Models strategies for future practice • Promotes participation of students • Challenges values and norms of each discipline	**For the Healthcare System** • Holds potential for more efficient delivery of care • Maximizes facilities and/or resources • Reduces burden on acute care facilities through increased preventative care • Facilitates efforts for continuous quality improvement

Using Clinical Judgment

Another reason why a CV nurse creates an individualized patient care plan is that it helps the nurse, and other members of the team, pull information from different scientific disciplines. The written plan allows for critical thinking and utilizes the nurse's clinical judgement to solve any problems that may arise. Thinking skills and information processing become effectively ingrained into professional nursing practice. In addition, it assists in faster response times to any acute changes that may occur in the cardiac/vascular patient's condition.

Formulating Outcomes

Health outcomes must be realistic (attainable), measurable, and time-referenced. Outcomes are broadly understood to include the following elements:

- Clinical disease progression measures

- Patient-reported health and functional status

- Patient satisfaction with quality of life and health status

- Satisfaction with services

- Costs of health services

In the past, quality assessment focused on clinical outcomes, such as disease-specific measures. However, this will not necessarily tell the medical professional very much about how the patient is functioning and if desired health outcomes have actually been achieved. In order to completely understand outcomes, it is necessary to ask the patient about outcomes such as their quality of life, health status and service satisfaction.

IOM Goal Components

According to the Institute of Medicine (IOM), when formulating goals for patient outcomes and health services, six essential components should be included. These are:

1. Patient Safety: Patients should not be harmed by health care services that are intended to be of benefit.

2. Effectiveness: The basis of effective care is scientific evidence that the proposed treatment will increase the chances of desired health outcomes.

3. Timeliness: Health care must meet a patient's needs in a timely manner. Failure to do so can result in denial of critically needed services, progression of health conditions and/or worsening of outcomes.

4. Patient Centered: Patient-centered care involves listening to the patient's individual needs, values and/or preferences in order to give high-quality care.

5. Efficiency: Any waste and/or inefficiency in the provision of health care services should be continuously identified and/or eliminated.

6. Equity: The health care system should benefit all individuals regardless of age, gender, race, ethnicity, and/or religion.

Pharmacology

One of the standard interventions performed by a cardiac/vascular nurse is the administration of medications as prescribed by the patient's doctor. The CV nurse must have knowledge of the pharmacology of cardiac/vascular drugs including their indications, mechanism of action (MOA), drug classifications, and compatibility. In addition, a CV nurse must have skills in:

- Administering prescribed cardiac/vascular medications safely, including the ongoing monitoring of vital signs and laboratory test values

- Monitoring the patient's response to medications including whether the patient is having the desired response, as well as observing if they are experiencing any adverse effects and allergic reactions

Drug Classifications, MOA, Indications, and Adverse/Allergic Reactions

There are eight broad categories of drugs that improve a patient's cardiac/vascular functioning.

Cardiac Glycosides and Phosphodiesterase (PDE) Inhibitors

Also known as inotropics, these drugs have a positive inotropic effect on the heart. This means that they increase cardiac output as well as the force of the heart's contractions.

Drug	Indications	Adverse Effects/Allergic Reactions	Nursing/Safety Considerations
Digoxin (Lanoxin) (Cardiac Glycoside)	supraventricular arrhythmias, heart failure	digoxin toxicity (e.g. nausea/vomiting, abdominal pain, headache, irritability, insomnia, depression), arrhythmias, anorexia, drowsiness	therapeutic dose = 0.5 – 2 ng/ml loading dose may be needed for immediate effect check apical pulse before giving – withhold and repeat pulse if < 60 bpm

Inamrinone (Inocor) (PDE Inhibitor)	heart failure difficult to treat with digoxin, diuretics, vasodilators, pt. awaiting heart transplant	arrhythmias, nausea, vomiting, headache, fever, chest pain, low potassium levels, low platelet levels	Contraindicated in acute phase of MI and/or after MI Potassium levels should be normal before/during therapy Only administered via IV
Milrinone (Primacor) (PDE Inhibitor)	heart failure difficult to treat with digoxin, diuretics, vasodilators, pt. awaiting heart transplant	arrhythmias, nausea, vomiting, headache, fever, chest pain, low potassium levels, low platelet levels	Contraindicated in acute phase of MI and/or after MI Potassium levels should be normal before/during therapy Only administered via IV

Antiarrhythmics

Antiarrhythmics are used to treat normal heart rhythm disturbances. They are subdivided into four classes and three sub-classes with different MOAs.

<u>Class 1A</u>

This class includes sodium channel blockers that control arrhythmias by altering the cell membrane of the myocardium and interfering with autonomic nervous system control of normal pacemaker.

Drug	Indications	Adverse Effects/Allergic Reactions	Nursing/Safety Considerations
Disopyramide (Norpace)	Ventricular tachycardia, atrial fibrillation, atrial flutter, paroxysmal atrial tachycardia	Diarrhea, nausea, vomiting, arrhythmias, ECG changes, liver damage, respiratory arrest	check apical pulse before giving – withhold if extreme – notify dr. use with caution in pt. with asthma
Procainamide (Procanbid)			
Quinidine Sulphate (Quinidex)			

Class 1B

This class works by blocking rapid influx of sodium ions during the depolarization phase of the depolarization/re-polarization cycle, which results in reduced refractory period reducing arrhythmia risk.

Drug	Indications	Adverse Effects/Allergic Reactions	Nursing/Safety Considerations
Lidocaine (Xylocaine) Mexiletine (Mexitil)	ventricular tachycardia and fibrillation	drowsiness, arrhythmias, hypotension, bradycardia, widened QRS complex	may increase effects of other antiarrhythmics administer via IV pump using infusion pump

Class 1C

Drugs in this class mainly slow the conduction system of the heart.

Drug	Indications	Adverse Effects/Allergic Reactions	Nursing/Safety Considerations
Flecainide (Tambocor) Moricizine (Ethmozine) Propafenone (Rythmol)	ventricular tachycardia and fibrillation, supraventricular arrhythmias	new arrhythmias, HF, cardiac death	correct electrolyte imbalances before administering monitor ECG before/after any dosage adjustments

Class 2

Drugs in this class include beta-adrenergic blockers, which slow automatic processes of the SA node, reduce conduction of AV node and pacer cells, and reduce the strength of heart contractions .

Drug	Indications	Adverse Effects/Allergic Reactions	Nursing/Safety Considerations
Acebutolol (Sectral) Esmolol (Brevibloc) Propranolol (Inderal)	atrial fibrillation/ flutter, paroxysmal atrial tachycardia, ventricular arrhythmias	arrhythmias, HF, bradycardia, hypotension, nausea/vomiting, bronchospasm	monitor apical HR and BP stopping abruptly can precipitate MI or exacerbate angina

Class 3

Class 3 drugs include exact MOA not known but thought to suppress arrhythmias by converting uni-directional block to a bi-directional block.

Drug	Indications	Adverse Effects/Allergic Reactions	Nursing/Safety Considerations
Amiodarone (Cordarone) Ibutilide Fumarate (Corvert)	Life threatening arrhythmias resistant to other antiarrhythmics	Aggravation of arrhythmias, hypotension, anorexia, severe pulmonary toxicity, liver dysfunction	Amiodarone increases risk of digoxin toxicity monitor HR and BP for any changes; monitor for signs of pulmonary toxicity in pts. taking Amiodarone

Class 4

This class includes calcium channel blockers, which block movement of calcium during phase 2 of action potential and slow conduction and refractory period of the calcium dependent tissues, including the AV node.

Drug	Indications	Adverse Effects/Allergic Reactions	Nursing/Safety Considerations
Diltiazem (Cardizem) Verapamil (Calan)	supraventricular arrhythmias	Peripheral edema, hypotension, anorexia, bradycardia, atrioventricular block, flushing (Diltiazem), HF, pulmonary edema	monitor HR/rhythm, BP carefully when initiating and/or changing dosage calcium supplements may decrease efficacy

Antianginals

There are three main types of antianginals that relieve chest pain associated with angina by increasing the supply of oxygen to the heart and decreasing the myocardium's demand for oxygen. These include nitrates, beta-adrenergic receptor blockers, and calcium channel blockers.

Nitrates

Drug	Indications	Adverse Effects/Allergic Reactions	Nursing/Safety Considerations
Isosorbide (Isodil) Isosorbide mononitrate (Imdur) Nitroglycerine (Nito-Bid)	prevention and/or relief of acute angina	hypotension, headache, dizziness, elevated HR	monitor BP before and after only use sublingual/translingual for acute angina avoid with pts. taking erectile dysfunction meds due to risk of severe hypotension

Beta-Adrenergic Receptor Blockers

Drug	Indications	Adverse Effects/Allergic Reactions	Nursing/Safety Considerations
Atenolol (Tenormin) Carvedilol (Coreg) Metoprolol (Lopressor)	long-term prevention of angina first line of therapy for hypertension stable HF caused by reduced left ventricular ejection fraction	bradycardia, fainting, fluid retention, HF, arrhythmias, nausea, diarrhea, atrioventricular blocks, hypoglycemia, bronchospasm	monitor apical pulse before monitor BP, HR, ECG and HR/rhythm often hypoglycemia may be masked – watch diabetes for sweating, fatigue, etc. monitor pts. with respiratory history for breathing problems

Calcium Channel Blockers

Drug	Indications	Adverse Effects/Allergic Reactions	Nursing/Safety Considerations
Amlodipine (Nonvasc) Diltiazem (Cardizem) Nifedipine (Adalat)	long-term prevention of angina hypertension	orthostatic hypotension, HF, hypotension, arrhythmias, headache, dizziness, persistent peripheral edema	monitor HR/rhythm, BP closely at first or when increasing dosage calcium supplements may reduce efficacy

Antihypertensives

Antihypertensives are used to reduce hypertension. The MOA is different for each drug, depending on the drug classification. These include:

- Sympatholytics: Inhibit sympathetic nervous system which causes dilation of peripheral blood vessels and lower BP.

- Vasodilators: Relax peripheral vascular smooth muscles causing dilation of vessels.

- Angiotensin-converting enzyme (ACE) inhibitors: Interrupt the renin-angiotensin-aldosterone system (RAAS).

- Angiotensin II receptor blockers (ARB): Inhibit action of angiotensin II by attaching to tissue binding receptor sites

Drug Classification	Indications	Adverse Effects/Allergic Reactions	Nursing/Safety Considerations
Sympatholytic Drugs			
Central-acting nervous system inhibitors: Clonidine (Catapres) Guanabenz (Wytensin) Guanfacine (Tenex) Methyldopa *Alpha Blockers:* Doxazosin (Cardural) Phentolamine (Regitine) Prazosin (Minipress) Terazosin (Hytrin) *Mixed alpha- and beta- adrenergic receptor blockers:* Labetalol (Normodynel) *Norepinephrine depletors:* Guanadrel (Hylorel)	hypertension	hypotension (alpha blockers), drowsiness, depression, edema, vertigo (central-acting drugs), bradycardia, hepatic necrosis, arrhythmias	monitor HR, BP before and after

Vasodilators

Diazoxide (Hyperstat I.V.) Hydralazine (Apresoline) Minoxidil Nitroprusside (Nitropress)	administered in combination with other drugs to treat moderate to severe hypertension hypertensive crisis	tachycardia, palpations, angina, headache, fatigue, severe pericardial effusion, hepatotoxicity, nausea, Stevens-Johnson syndrome	monitor HR, BP before and after monitor pts. receiving nitroprusside for cyanide toxicity

Angiotensin-Converting Enzyme (ACE) Inhibitors

Benazepril (Lotensin) Captopril (Capoten) Enalapril (Vasotec) Lisinopril (Prinivil) Quinapril (Accupril)	primary/secondary hypertension HF	angioedema, persistent cough, rash, renal insufficiency, hypotension, nausea/vomiting	monitor BP and pulse before and after administering monitor WBC/electrolytes

Angiotensin II Receptor Blockers

Candesartan (Atacand) Irbesartan (Avapro) losartan (Cozaar) Olmesartan (Benicar) Valsartan (Diovan)	hypertension, HF that is resistant to ACE inhibitors	hypotension, fatigue, abdominal pain, rash	Monitor BP and pulse before and after administering

Diuretics

Diuretics are used to treat various C/V diseases – MOA promotes excretion of H2O and electrolytes by kidneys.

Drug Classification	Indications	Adverse Effects/Allergic Reactions	Nursing/Safety Considerations
Thiazine and Thiazine-like Diuretics			
Bendroflume-thiazide (Naturetin) Chlorthalidone (Hygroton) Hydrochlorothiazide (HydroDIURIL) Hydroflume-thiazide (Saluron) Indapamide (Lozol) Methyclothiazide (Enduron)	hypertension, edema	hypokalemia, orthostatic hypotension, hyponatremia, nausea, dizziness	monitor potassium levels Monitor I/O Monitor glucose levels in diabetic patients as thiazide diuretics can cause hyperglycemia
Loop Diuretics			
Bumetanide (Bumex) Ethacrynic acid (Edecrin) Furosemide (Lasix)	hypertension, HF, edema	dehydration, orthostatic hypotension, dizziness, hyperuricemia, hypokalemia, hyponatremia, muscle cramps, rash	monitor for signs of excess diuresis monitor BP, HR, I/O monitor electrolyte levels
Potassium-Sparing Diuretics			
Amiloride (Midamor) Spironolactone (Aldactone) Triamterene (Dyrenium)	Edema, diuretic-induced hypokalemia in patients with HF, cirrhosis, hypertension, nephritic syndrome	hyperkalemia, headache, nausea, rash	monitor ECG for arrhythmias monitor potassium levels monitor I/O

Anticoagulants

Anticoagulants are used to reduce blood's clotting ability. The MOA is different for each drug, depending on the drug classification.

- Heparins: Inhibit formation of fibrin and thrombin by activating antithrombin III, which inactivates certain factors in the intrinsic and common pathways preventing stable clot formation.

- Oral anticoagulants: Alter liver's ability to synthesize vitamin K-dependent clotting factors such as prothrombin.

- Antiplatelet drugs: Interfere with activity of platelets by decreasing sticking/clumping in the blood.

Drug Classification	Indications	Adverse Effects/Allergic Reactions	Nursing/Safety Considerations
Heparins			
Dalteparin (Fragmin) Enoxaparin (Lovenox)	deep vein thrombosis(DVT), embolism prevention, disseminated intravascular coagulation (heparin), prevention of MI complications	bleeding, hemorrhage, thrombocytopenia	obtain prothrombin time (PT) and International Normalized Ratio (INR) levels before giving monitor thromboplastin time; range is 1.5 to 2.5 times the control monitor pt. for signs of bleeding administration with nonsteroidal anti-inflammatory drugs, iron dextran or an antiplatelet drug increases bleeding risks

Oral Anticoagulants:			
Warfarin (Coumadin)	deep vein thrombosis prevention, prevent complications of prosthetic heart valves or diseased mitral valves, atrial arrhythmias	bleeding (may be severe), diarrhea, hepatitis	monitor PT and INR before/during/after INR should be 90-140 monitor for signs of bleeding effects of oral anti-coagulants can be reversed with Vitamin K
Antiplatelet Drugs			
Aspirin (Ecotrin) Dipyridamole (Persantine) Ticlopidine (Ticlid) Clopididogrel (Plavix)	Preventative for heart attack and stroke decrease risk of death post-MI prevent complications of prosthetic heart valves reduce MI risk following previous MI or in unstable angina pts prevent reocclusion in coronary revascularization procedures	GI distress, bleeding, thrombocytopenia, angioedema, palpitations	monitor for signs of bleeding Aspirin and ticlopidine should be taken with meals to prevent GI irritation Dipyridamole should be taken with a full glass of fluid minimum of 1 hour before meals safety measures to reduce bleeding risks (e.g. soft toothbrush, electric razor) (Brennan et al., 2008; Tanner, 2013)

Thrombolytics

Thrombolytics are "clot busters" that dissolve pre-existing clots within an artery by converting plasminogen to plasmin resulting in dissolution of thrombi, fibrinogen, and other plasma proteins.

Drug	Indications	Adverse Effects/Allergic Reactions	Nursing/Safety Considerations
Alteplase (Activase)	acute MI	bleeding, allergic reactions	monitor PTT, PT, INR, hemoglobin, hematocrit before/during/after
Reteplase (Retavase)	acute ischemic stroke		monitor punctures sites for bleeding
Streptokinase (Streptase)	pulmonary emboli		monitor for bleeding
	arterial thrombosis		don't use tourniquet when drawing blood
	catheter occulsion		safety measures to reduce bleeding risks (e.g. soft toothbrush, electric razor)

Antilipemics

Antilipemics are used in combination with changes in lifestyle (e.g. diet, exercise) to reduce levels of serum cholesterol, triglycerides and phospholipids. MOA depends on drug classification:

- Bile sequestering drugs: Remove excessive bile acids from fat deposits and reduce levels of low-density lipoprotein (LDL).

- Fibric-acid derivatives: MOA not exactly known but lower triglyceride levels and increase HDL minimally.

- HMG-CoA reductase inhibitors (statins): Interfere with synthesis of cholesterol by inhibiting enzymes responsible for changing HMG-CoA to mevolonate.

- Cholesterol absorption inhibitors: Inhibit cholesterol absorption from intestines - leading to reduction in delivery of cholesterol from the intestines to the liver – increase clearance of cholesterol from the blood.

Drug Classification	Indications	Adverse Effects/Allergic Reactions	Nursing/Safety Considerations
Bile-Sequestering Drugs			
Cholestyramine (Questran) Colesevelam (Welcho) Colestipol (Colestid)	elevated cholesterol levels	constipation, increased tendency to bleed, muscle/joint pain, nausea, heartburn, headaches	instruct pt of need to return for periodic blood tests give before meals don't give the powder form dry; mix with fluids give other drugs 1 hour before or 4 to 6 hours afterwards

Fibric Acid Derivatives			
Fenofibrate (Tricor) Gemfibrozil (Lopid)	high cholesterol high triglycerides	rash, nausea/vomiting, diarrhea, myalgia, flu-like syndrome, impotence, dizziness, blurred vision, abdominal and/or epigastric pain	instruct pt of need to return for periodic blood tests educate re dietary/lifestyle changes to help lower cholesterol/ triglyceride levels administer with meals
HMG-CoA Reductase Inhibitors (Statins)			
Atorvastatin (Lipitor) Fluvastatin (Lescol) Lovastatin (Mevacor) Pravastatin (Pravachol) Simvastatin (Zocor) Rosuvastatin (Crestor)	elevated cholesterol, triglyceride, and LDL levels prevention of C/V disease in adults without clinical evidence of coronary disease but multiple risk factors	rhabdomyolysis (i.e. muscle wasting disease) with acute renal failure, headache, flatulence, abdominal pain, constipation, nausea	instruct pt. of need to return for periodic blood tests monitor liver function tests periodically report any unexplained muscle weakness/soreness give at the same time each day doesn't need to be given with food educate the patient on dietary/lifestyle changes to help lower cholesterol/ triglyceride levels
Cholesterol Absorption Inhibitors			
Ezetimibe (Zetia)	elevated cholesterol, triglycerides and LDL levels given as adjunct with Simvastatin	cough, myalgia, arthralgia, dizziness, headache	instruct pt. to return for blood tests educate the patient on dietary/lifestyle changes to help lower cholesterol/ triglyceride levels

Polypharmacy

Polypharmacy is the practice of prescribing at least four medications to the same patient. This tends to occur in older patients who have concurrent diseases where every condition requires a specific medication regiment. Those patients who suffer from medical conditions, such as diabetes and hypertension, are also at an increased risk for ischemic heart disease, cardiovascular disease, and stroke.

When it comes to managing a patient's multiple health problems, doctors often find it quite a challenge as they weigh the necessity of treating common conditions while still avoiding various polypharmacy risks such as an alteration of the patient's biophysiology, adverse reactions and/or drug to drug interactions. Possible effects of altered biophysiology include an older patient not being capable of tolerating certain prescribed medications in the normal therapeutic dosages.

The elderly can also experience various adverse effects such as decreased salivary production. Some medication combinations can result in confusion which puts these patients at an increased risk for falls and other injuries. For these reasons, it is extremely important that a C/V nurse possess knowledge of possible drug to drug interactions as well as the ability to act accordingly.

Digoxin Interactions

Medications that Increase Digoxin Concentration in a C/V Patient's Bloodstream:

- Quinidine
- Verapamil
- Diltiazem
- Amiodarone
- Carvedilol
- Omeprazole (Prilosec)
- Propafenone
- Spironoloactone

Medications that may Decrease Heart Rate and AV Conduction

- Verapamil
- Diltiazem
- Amiodarone
- Beta Blockers
- Propafenone
- Sotalol

Medications that may Decrease Absorption of Digoxin

- Antacids
- Cholestyramine
- Colestipol

Warfarin (Coumadin) Interactions

Medications that can Decrease INR or Increase Risks for Clotting

- Barbiturates
- Binding Resins
- Carbamazepine (Tegretol)
- Oral Contraceptives
- Penicillin
- Rifampin – if use can't be avoided, consider increasing Coumadin dosage by 25-40%
- Vitamin K

Medications that can have Variable Effects on INR or Risk for Bleeding

- Allopurinol
- Corticosteroids
- Phenytoin (Dilantin)

Role of Nurses and Pharmacists in Polypharmacy

There are several ways that nurses and pharmacists can contribute to the reduction of polypharmacy in patients. Some practical measures include:

- Supporting self-administration of medications while still in hospital.

- Evaluating/monitoring how patients take their prescribed medications.

- Constantly being alert to any unexpected drug to drug interactions and/or adverse effects.

- Giving patients various written materials that complement any pharmaceutical leaflets. These materials should have larger print and/or good color contrast for use by those who have vision issues.

- Confirming that the patient understands as well as agrees to a prescribed medication regiment.

- Counseling concerning any changes in lifestyle that might decrease the necessity for medication(s) as well as any potential adverse effects of required medications.

There is a distinct possibility that polypharmacy may take place upon discharge from hospital as a result of poor communication between the patient's primary and secondary care providers. When a CV patient is discharged, any pertinent information that is sent to the family doctor, long term care facility, family members and caregivers must clearly indicate whether the medication list is a replacement for, or an addition to, any previously prescribed medications

Drug to Food Interactions

While healthy eating is very important in the ongoing treatment of all cardiac/vascular diseases, certain foods, including healthy choices, can reduce the effectiveness of some cardiovascular medications. There are certain fruits and vegetables that can cause unintended and/or dangerous interactions with various CV drugs.

Statins and Grapefruit/Pomegranates

When patients eat either grapefruits or pomegranates while taking some statin-based cholesterol medications such as atorvastatin (Lipitor), lovastatin (Mevacor), and simvastatin (Zocor), it can be a dangerous mix. If cardiac/vascular patients really enjoy eating these fruits they can be treated with alternative cholesterol medications like rosuvastatin (Crestor).

Warfarin and Leafy Greens

As a result of high levels of Vitamin K contained in green leafy vegetables such as spinach or kale, they can pose potential risks in cardiac/vascular patients who take warfarin (Coumadin) to prevent blood clots and/or strokes. Eating excessive amounts of these types of vegetables can counteract the effectiveness of warfarin.

There needs to be a careful balance and adjustments made to an individual's diet when taking Warfarin. For example, if a patient is used to eating salad three days per week, he or she should continue to do so in order to maintain proper balance and consistency. Cardiac/vascular patients need to be aware of any potential interactions between different drugs and/or foods as well as maintain ongoing communication with their healthcare providers.

Herbal Therapy and Drug Interactions

A CV nurse must also have knowledge of any herbal supplements that cardiac/vascular patients may take in addition to their prescription medications. These herbal compounds may interact with cardiovascular medications in adverse ways. For example, herbals may either decrease or intensify the therapeutic effect of a prescription medication. In extreme cases, the combination might be toxic and cause significant harm to the patient.

It is the CV nurse's responsibility to question whether a patient is taking any herbal supplements during the course of the initial cardiac/vascular patient history on admission to hospital. This information should be noted and shared with other members of the interdisciplinary team.

Feverfew

- Used to prevent/treat migraine headaches, fever and/or arthritis.
- Should not be taken with Aspirin, Coumadin, NSAIDS, thrombolytics and antiplatelet medications, as doing so results in prolonged bleeding times.

Ginseng

- Considered to be an anti-inflammatory
- Possesses estrogen effects
- Enhances the immune system
- Improves physical and mental abilities
- Reduces anticoagulant and NSAID therapeutic effects
- Do not administer with corticosteroids – may cause higher levels
- High dosages of ginseng can cause liver issues

Gingko

- Used to improve memory and/or to treat depression
- Thought to improve peripheral circulation
- Should not be taken with antiplatelet, anticoagulant and/or MAO Inhibitor medications
- Elevates patient's bleeding time, if taken along with NSAIDS

Echinacea

- Used to treat colds, fevers and UTIs
- Can interfere with immunosuppressant drugs as well as intensify, dilute and/or exacerbate the adverse effects of heart medications including blood thinners and/or cholesterol-lowering statins
- No reputable scientific evidence has found Echinacea to be effective in treating colds, fevers or UTIs in thirty years of studying the compound

Kava Kava

- Used to treat muscle pains/aches and mild insomnia
- Can increase effects of CNS suppressants

St. John's Wort

- Used to treat mild depression.

- Can increase adverse CNS effects when used in combination with antidepressants and/or alcohol.

Ma Huang

- Used for weight loss, improving overall energy levels and to treat hay fever and asthma

- Increases the effects of cardiac glycosides, theophylline, and MAO Inhibitors

Evaluation (18%)

Care Plan Revisions

Determining a cardiac/vascular patient's overall progress, by evaluating the effectiveness of nursing care interventions, is vital to the patient's recovery and optimal long term prognosis. The cardiac/vascular nurse will have already designed and implemented an individualized care plan upon a patient's admission to the hospital, and continued it right up until their discharge. Ideally, this plan will be:

- Patient-focused
- Coordinated
- Collaborative
- Evidence-based
- Cost-effective

As part of the continuous evaluation process, the cardiac/vascular nurse should have sufficient knowledge of the anticipated outcomes of prescribed clinical cardiac/vascular interventions. He or she also needs to have the skills necessary to re-assess and interpret any observable patterns and variances related to an individual patient's response to prescribed interventions. The nurse utilizes the gathered information to update the patient-specific plan of care, as warranted.

Utilizing various evaluation tools, discussed in detail in earlier sections, the cardiac/vascular nurse continuously monitors and evaluates a CV patient's response (or lack of response) to prescribed nursing interventions. As the patient transitions through the various stages of illness, healing, and recovery, their continuity of care is facilitated by:

- Careful, detailed documentation
- Updates to patient care plan to reflect any changes in status
- Ongoing planning for eventual discharge to either the patient's own home or another care facility
- Clearly written, detailed instructions for hospital discharge
- Effective, two-way communication with outpatient and/or next level patient care setting(s)

Discharge Planning

Ultimately, a cardiac/vascular nurse is required to assist their patients in the achievement of a smooth hospital discharge and a seamless transition to either their own home or another healthcare facility. The CV nurse needs to possess an adequate level of knowledge in two specific discharge planning areas as well as skills in two other areas:

1. Cost-effective treatment options including choices of medications (lower priced generics) and left ventricular assist devices (LVADs) which are covered by most medical insurance plans.

2. Resources available to the CV patient. These include curative care, palliative care, end of life care, short-term and/or long-term cardiac/vascular rehabilitation, as well as community resources, such as in-person and/or online support groups.

3. Setting priorities and planning for continuing patient care.

4. Encouraging ongoing patient adherence to medication schedules, diet/lifestyle changes, cardiac/vascular rehabilitation programs, etc.

Cost-Effective Treatment Options

Generic Drugs

In the U.S., close to 80 percent of medication prescriptions are filled using generic drugs. This trend is predicted to be ongoing. Many patients and their health care providers continue to look for lower, more cost-effective treatment options for many medical conditions including cardiac/vascular diseases and disorders.

Many cardiac/vascular patients are older retirees who are on fixed incomes. Hence, generic drugs are more affordable treatment options for them. The following are a few important facts to note concerning generic drugs as compared to brand name medications.

- Quality – Generic drugs must have the same quality and performance as brand name drugs according to FDA regulations. In order to be FDA approved, generic drugs must met rigorous standards of identity, quality, strength, potency, and purity. While a certain degree of variability occurs during the manufacturing process, in both brand name and generic drugs, the FDA limits the amount of accepted variability.

- Activity – Generic drugs must contain the same active ingredient(s), dosage form(s), strength, and administration routes as their brand name counterparts. However, generics do not necessarily have to contain exactly the same inactive ingredients.

- Standards – All generic manufacturing, packaging, and sites for testing have to pass the same exacting specifications and quality standards as brand name drugs. In fact, several generic drugs are manufactured in the same plants as brand name products.

- Research – Current research indicates that generic drugs work just as well as brand name products do. Published results from 38 different clinical trials, comparing cardiovascular generic drugs to their brand name counterparts, indicate that there is no significant evidence that brand name CV drugs work any better than their generic counterparts do.

- Efficacy – The FDA does NOT allow a 45 percent difference in the efficacy of generic drug products. A generic product, modeled after a brand name drug, has to perform in more or less the same way within the body as the brand name equivalent does. While not medically significant, there will always be a slight degree of naturally occurring variability.

- Price – Typically, generic drugs are 80 to 85 percent lower in price. However, cheaper does not mean lower levels of quality. Manufacturers of generic drugs can sell their drug products for less because they do not have to repeat costly clinical trials of new drugs. Generally, they do not pay for expensive advertising and marketing promotions. Often, more than one generic company is FDA-approved to manufacture/market a single generic product, creating market competition, which can result in lowering of prices.

- FDA monitoring – Both brand name and generic drugs are monitored for adverse events by the FDA. This is one aspect of the FDA overall efforts to evaluate the safety of drugs following approval. Often, adverse event reports actually describe an already known reaction to a drug's active ingredient. As appropriate, reports are actively investigated, potentially leading to changes in the ways either generic and/or brand name products are manufactured and/or used.

Left Ventricular Assist Devices (LVADs)

A left ventricular assist device, also known as an LVAD, is a mechanical "pump-type" unit that is operated by an external battery and control system. It is surgically implanted into the cardiac/vascular patient's chest cavity assisting in the maintenance of the heart's pumping ability when it cannot function effectively on its own. Typically, an LVAD has a tube which pulls blood out of the lower left chamber and into a pump which then sends the blood into the aorta. This action effectively helps the deteriorating left ventricle. Portable LVADs are often used for weeks to months. Therefore, patients can be discharged from the hospital with the potential of having an acceptable quality of life while waiting for a donor heart.

Sometimes referred to as a "bridge to transplant," an LVAD basically functions as an artificial heart. It can be utilized in longer-term therapy as cardiac patients often wait for very long periods before suitable donor hearts become available. During this time period, the patient's heart may deteriorate and weaken even further. It can become incapable of pumping sufficient blood to keep the patient alive. Thus, it is possible that an LVAD might actually eliminate the need for a heart transplant.

Recently, LVADs have been used as "destination therapies" in cases of heart failure patients where transplants are not considered viable options. According to the American Heart Association, LVADs can reduce the risk of death in patients with end-stage HF by as much as 50 percent, at six and twelve months, and extend their average life span from approximately three months to over ten months. In the US, LVADs are reimbursable by the Center for Medicare and Medicaid Services as well as most private insurance companies. The majority of insurance plans will also cover the costs associated with maintenance equipment and driveline dressing supplies.

LVAD Patient Teaching Before Discharge

Before a cardiac/vascular patient with an LVAD device is discharged from the hospital, the C/V nurse should instruct them on certain facts. These include:

- Immediately inform the cardiac/vascular specialist about signs and symptoms of infection including any redness, swelling, and/or drainage at the incision site as well as the occurrence of any fever or chest pain.

- Immediately inform the cardiac/vascular specialist about signs and symptoms of HF such as dyspnea, weight gain, and/or edema.

- Follow prescribed medication regimen, reporting any adverse reactions or side effects.

- Follow prescribed low sodium, low fat diet.

- Balance activity and rest periods appropriately.

- If prescribed, adhere to exercise and rehabilitation programs.

- Adhere to laboratory schedule for monitoring of INR blood levels, if on warfarin.

Curative and Palliative Care

Cardiac/vascular patients can sometimes find living with their cardiac/vascular condition extremely difficult. They can experience a great deal of pain as well as feelings of loneliness, anger, fear, anxiety, and depression. Often they think that their treatment(s) are actually doing more harm than good. Palliative care can help CV patients, their loved ones and/or caregivers cope with their condition and related experiences and emotions. Designed for those patients who have serious illnesses or diseases, it is different from curative care. The latter is defined as health care typically aimed at obtaining a cure for an existing disease and/or medical condition so that the patient can live longer.

Purpose of Palliative Care

The main focus of palliative care is to improve a patient's overall quality of life including their mind and spirit. It is possible to combine palliative and curative care. For example, heart failure patients can benefit from palliative care while they are receiving treatment for their cardiac condition. Any type of care provided to cardiac/vascular patients is needs-dependent with specific goals guiding the care that is given. Palliative care can:

- Reduce levels of pain and/or side effects of treatments.

- Help patients, their loved ones, and caregivers understand their specific CV disease better.

- Assist patients in talking about the feelings they are experiencing more openly.

- Help patients make informed decisions concerning treatments they do, or do not, want to undergo.

- Assist in ongoing communication between patients, doctors, nurses and loved ones.

Working closely with other doctors, in order to give the best care possible, palliative care providers try to ensure that a CV patient's medical care is meeting the needs of their mind, body and spirit. Palliative care providers also assist patients in formulating plans for future medical and health care.

Palliative Care Team

Palliative care involves active participation of cardiac/vascular patients and their families. They work with health care providers in doctors' offices, their homes, hospitals, nursing home and/or hospices. Today, many hospitals have palliative care teams that can include:

- Palliative care doctors
- Nurses
- Social workers
- Spiritual advisors
- Occupational therapists
- Pharmacists
- Respiratory therapists
- Physical therapists
- Dieticians/nutritionists
- Volunteers

Palliative Care Concerns

During the course of a palliative care visit, the following concerns can be addressed:

- Treatments
- Pain
- Adverse effects of prescribed medications
- Emotional and/or social challenges and help with family conflicts
- Spiritual issues
- Goals
- Need for end of life (hospice) care
- Advanced healthcare directives – These are instructions given to a patient's doctor and loved ones concerning the type of care desired if the patient becomes unable to speak for him or herself. These types of directives include "do not resuscitate," "do not intubate," and "no ventilator support"

End of Life Care

End of life, also known as hospice, care provides medical services, emotional support and/or spiritual resources for patients who are in the final stages of any type of serious disease or illness, such as severe heart failure, cancer, or end-stage COPD. Typically, end of life care is intended for patients who are not expected to live for more than six months.

Patients face many difficult decisions as they near the end of their lives, including the type of care they want to be given, where they want to receive care as well as who to assign to make decisions for them, if they are not able to do so. Dying patients need lots of time and assistance to plan their end of life care including issues such as:

- Life-sustaining measures – Includes whether they desire certain "heroic" measures to be taken in order to keep them alive, such as CPR or insertion of a ventilator tube, should their heart and/or breathing stop.

- Advanced directives – Discussing and informing their family members what they want and/or have already decided concerning medical care and/or legal matters. They should consider writing an advanced directive which includes a "living will," as well as a medical "power of attorney" (durable power of attorney). Living wills are legal documents that express specific medical care wishes. A medical power of attorney allows a person to choose a health care agent. Whomever is delegated the patient's health care agent has the legal right to make medical treatment decisions on behalf of the patient at the end of life or anytime the patient is incapable of speaking on their own behalf.

- Organ donation – Whether they would like to donate their organs for medical and research purposes.

- End of life care – Where they want to receive end of life care. Some individuals chose to be cared for within a hospital setting while others choose to be taken care of in their own homes or a nursing home.

- Hospice care – Another option is a hospice center where patients can get much needed emotional and/or spiritual support. Generally, the costs of hospice care are covered by Medicare, Medicaid and/or private insurance plans. If patients have no coverage, hospice administration typically work with patients and/or their relatives to ensure that patients receive the individualized care they require as they near the end of their life.

Cardiac/Vascular Rehabilitation

According to the World Health Organization (WHO), cardiac/vascular rehabilitation is defined as "the sum of activities required to ensure cardiac patients the best possible physical, mental and social conditions so that they may, by their own efforts, resume and maintain as normal a place as possible in the community."

The majority of cardiac/vascular patients can lower their risks for future heart problems if they make conscious lifestyle changes to improve their overall health. In partnership with their cardiovascular specialist, family doctor, nurses, pharmacists and/or other healthcare professionals, cardiac/vascular patients can play an active role in effecting long-term lifestyle changes. Also, patients should take an active role in their own health care by knowing their short-term and long-term goals, making positive changes in their health habits and taking their medications as prescribed, as well as acting quickly in the event of either new or worsening signs/symptoms.

Cardiac rehabilitation is a professionally supervised program which assists cardiac/vascular patients in recovering from various types of conditions and/or diseases including myocardial infarctions, heart surgeries, and percutaneous coronary intervention procedures (PCI) including angioplasty (a procedure used to open a clogged artery), and stenting, which involves permanent insertion of a small wire mesh tube into an artery to reduce the chances of further narrowing.

In addition, cardiac rehabilitation programs typically offer cardiovascular education and counseling services to assist patients in increasing their individual levels of physical fitness and reduce persistent cardiac symptoms, such as blood pressure, cholesterol and lipid levels. This program is useful for improving overall physical and mental health through diet, weight control, and stress management and to reduce the risks of future cardiac/vascular events, thus extending life.

While participating in a cardiac rehab program, a cardiac/vascular patient receives advice and close supervision from various healthcare professionals who regularly communicate with their primary health care doctor and/or cardiac specialist. All aged individuals who suffer from cardiac/vascular conditions can benefit from participating in a cardiac rehab program. These programs are used for patients with the following conditions:

- Heart attack
- Coronary artery disease (CAD)
- Heart Failure (HF)
- Angina
- Coronary artery bypass graft (CABG) surgery

- Coronary angioplasty (balloon angioplasty)

- Stenting

- Valve replacement

- Pacemaker insertion

- Implantable cardioverter defibrillator (ICD)

Length of Cardiac Rehab Programs

Cardiac rehab plans are "needs driven" depending on the individual patient. Some patients only attend rehab for six weeks. Other cardiac/vascular patients require six months, or even longer, to learn to effectively manage their conditions as well as develop healthier habits. Many short-term cardiac rehab programs continue for three months while long-term programs may last for years.

Components of Cardiac Rehabilitation Programs

- A medical evaluation – This is done in order to determine a patient's individual needs and/or limitations. This information is used to set goals and to customize a rehabilitation program.

- A physical activity program – One of these is designed to fit a cardiac/vascular patient's specific needs. Training generally begins within a group setting where the patient's heart rate and blood pressure are monitored while taking part in physical tasks. Patients work with physical therapists, exercise physiologists, and other healthcare professionals. Cardiac rehab participants are taught how to check their own heart rates and activity intensity levels. Eventually, patients undergo more strenuous aerobic activities such as using exercise bikes and/or treadmills.

- Cardiac education and counseling – This is done to assist a patient in both understanding and managing their own cardiac/vascular condition. Dietitians create individualized healthy eating plans for patients and educate them accordingly. Other healthcare professionals counsel patients on health issues such as smoking cessation and coping strategies to deal with stress, anger and/or depression during cardiac recovery.

- Training and support – This is done to assist patients in returning to work and/or performing other normal day to day activities.

Phases of Cardiac Rehabilitation Programs

Generally, there are at least three to four phases of cardiac rehab. These include:

- Phase I: Begins in hospital with the gradual resumption of activities of daily living as well as walking, stair climbing and range of motion exercises.

- Phase II: Starts after discharge from the hospital and is normally done within an outpatient setting. Phase II includes gradually increased levels of exercises plus other services that often include stress management, nutritional and/or smoking cessation counseling.

- Phase III/Phase IV: Emphasizes a long-term maintenance and conditioning program to follow for the rest of the patient's life. Cardiac rehab patients may use their own exercise routine at home, at a local gym or possibly continue their exercise programs at a local cardiac rehab center.

Choosing a Cardiac Rehabilitation Program

Most cardiac rehab programs are covered by private medical insurance plans and Medicare for two or three months. When choosing a particular program, a patient should take the following factors into consideration:

- Time: Is the program run at a time that is convenient for their schedule?

- Location: Is the program close to home and/or easy to access?

- Services: Does the program offer the specific services required?

- Setting: Does the program include group and/or individual services? Will the majority of the physical activity be performed at the cardiac rehab facility or at home?

- Cost: Can he or she afford the program being considered? Is it covered by the patient's own private medical insurance plan and/or by Medicare?

Community Resources

Local cardiac support groups are typically offered in area medical centers, community centers and/or on the Internet. Cardiac/vascular patients often find coping with a heart or vascular condition extremely challenging. They are often in physical pain, feel lonely, angry, frightened, anxious, and depressed. Joining either an in-person or online cardiac patient support group can help patients adjust to living with their particular cardiac/vascular condition and recuperate from a heart attack, cardiac procedure, or other surgery. Patients will be able to communicate with others who are experiencing or have experienced the same kinds of:

- Cardiac condition(s)
- Physical/mental symptom(s)
- Procedures or surgeries
- Ways to best perform everyday activities

Setting Priorities and Planning for Continuing Patient Care after Discharge

Heart Failure (HF)

Prior to discharge from hospital, the CV nurse should educate the patient. This involves advising and teaching the heart failure patient to:

- Take the radial pulse for one minute and then record it in a home journal to show to the doctor when going for follow-up appointments
- Report important signs and symptoms including loss of appetite, dizziness, shortness of breath, blurred vision, dry cough that persists, palpitations, increased levels of fatigue, swollen ankles/legs/feet, decreased output of urine, and increased nightly urination.
- Obtain personal weight three times (or more) per week. Keep a record and report 3-5 pound gains in one week to their doctor
- Follow a low sodium and high potassium diet as instructed by the doctor or dietician. Show the patient how to read nutritional labels on food items

Coronary Artery Disease (CAD)

Prior to discharge from hospital, the CV nurse must provide education to patients. This involves teaching the patient to:

- Report any recurring symptoms of angina to their doctor since they may be an indication of re-obstruction following procedures such as percutaneous transluminal coronary angioplasty (PTCA)
- Identify and avoid specific activities that appear to precipitate angina episodes

- Choose more appropriate mechanisms to cope with stressful situations to reduce the likelihood of angina symptoms.

- Consider changing jobs if their occupation is a constant source of fatigue, angina episodes, and stress

- Assure the patient that he or she will be able to resume sexual activities and that certain modifications can alleviate any fear of angina pain or the possibility of re-occlusion

- Register for a cardiac rehab program close to home that meets their cardiac needs or limitations

- Stop smoking immediately or never start again, and register for a local smoking cessation program

Acute Coronary Syndrome (ACS)

Prior to discharge from hospital, the CV nurse should advise and teach the ACS patient regarding his or her condition. This includes these instructions:

- Alternate periods of activity and rest

- Avoid the cold

- Control stress levels

- Participate in a stepped cardiac rehabilitation program

- Progressively resume sexual activity, but may need to take nitroglycerine beforehand to avoid angina symptoms

- Report any chest pain (typical or atypical) to the CV nurse or physician

- Stop smoking immediately and never start again, and refer to a local smoking cessation program.

- Discuss an appropriate diet with a hospital dietician including foods to avoid

Peripheral Artery Disease (PAD)

Prior to discharge from hospital, the CV nurse should advise and teach the PAD patient regarding his or her condition. This includes these instructions:

- Watch for any recurring signs and signs such as pain, pallor, numbness, paralysis, and/or absence of pulse

- Avoid wearing any constrictive clothing (e.g. garters), crossing their legs and/or accidently bumping affected limbs

- Avoid extremes in temperature. Dress warmly when going out into the cold. Especially, keep feet warm

- Wear properly fitting shoes and seek the care of a podiatrist for any foot problems

- Stop smoking immediately

- Perform foot care daily. Report any signs of infection and/or injuries to their doctor

- Discuss an appropriate diet with a hospital dietician including foods to avoid.

- Exercise regularly

Encouraging Ongoing Patient Adherence

Heart Failure (HF)

Prior to discharge from hospital, encourage the heart failure patient's ongoing adherence to:

- Taking prescribed heart failure medications, such as digoxin, as these drugs should be taken at the same time each day.

- Checking pulse rate/rhythm before taking medication and notifying the HCP if the pulse rate is < 60 bpm or if the rhythm is irregular.

- Following prescribed low sodium or high potassium diet based on their specific medication regime.

- Avoiding excessive fatigue by scheduling activities interspersed with rest periods.

Coronary Artery Disease (CAD)

- Following their prescribed medication regimen

- Following the prescribed low sodium and/or low-calorie diet

- Following their regular, moderate exercise plan

- Consistently attending cardiac rehab program

- Consistently attending smoking cessation program

Acute Coronary Syndrome (ACS)

- Following his or her prescribed medication regimen and other treatment methods

- Carrying nitroglycerine tablets, if ordered

- Reporting any adverse side effects from medications including anorexia, nausea/vomiting, vertigo, depression, and blurred vision

- Following prescribed low-sodium, low-fat, and low-cholesterol diet

- Consistently attending cardiac rehab program

- Regularly adhering to a smoking cessation program

- Keeping all follow-up cardiac testing and/or procedure appointments as well as any scheduled office visits with their PCP and/or cardiac/vascular specialist

Peripheral Artery Disease (PAD)

- Consistently attending smoking cessation program, if necessary.

- Following prescribed low-fat diet and maintaining a healthy weight.

- Following the prescribed exercise program.

- Following daily foot care regimen and avoiding tight clothing and/or shoes

Education (17%)

As the cardiac/vascular patient transitions along various CV care settings, ongoing, effective communication between the patient, family, caregivers, and members of the interdisciplinary team is vital. This includes having an appropriate, individualized cardiac/vascular education plan. The cardiac/vascular nurse is required to have knowledge of the components of this focused education plan, including pre-procedural and post-procedural education.

The cardiac/vascular nurse needs to identify the functional status and limitations of certain types of patients, such as amputees and stroke patients. A CV nurse also needs to assess and validate the patient's learning needs, readiness to learn, educational barriers, and literacy level. Lastly, the nurse must establish goals for the focused cardiac/vascular education plan and develop appropriate presentations for targeted audiences based on their learning styles and preferences.

The Education Plan

A clear, organized patient education and counseling plan is crucial to achieving optimal outcomes in any cardiac/vascular patient. A specific cardiac/vascular condition overview, associated signs and symptoms, dietary recommendations, activities, medication information, and exercise programs are taught to both patients and their families.

Since much of the information provided to patients is relatively complex, the interdisciplinary team approach can be quite useful in assisting patients to understand and remember information concerning their treatment regimen. Primary care providers, cardiologists, vascular specialists, cardiac/vascular nurses, home health nurses, dietitians, and/or pharmacists all play important roles in patient education. Written materials, CDs, DVDs are other valuable resources for patient education but should only be utilized as adjuncts, not as replacements for individualized in-person education.

The following is an example of suggested topics for the education and counseling of heart failure patients. This list can also be extended to other cardiac/vascular conditions:

- General topics
- Explanation of condition
- Expected symptoms vs. symptoms of worsening condition
- Psychological/mental/emotional responses

- Self-monitoring (daily weights)

- Plan of action in case of increased and/or worsening symptoms

- Prognosis (short-term vs. long-term)

- Pre-procedural and post-procedural expectations

- Advanced directives, such as living wills and powers of attorneys

- Diet plan

- Fluid restrictions

- Sodium restrictions

- Alcohol/caffeine restrictions

- Strategies for compliance to diet and lifestyle modification plan

- Activity/exercise programs and compliance strategy

- Work/leisure activities and compliance strategy

- Sexual activity

- Prescribed medications, such as nature of drugs, dosing, side effects, coping with complicated drug regimen, compliance strategy, and cost issues

Identifying Functional Status and Limitations in Certain Patient Types

Amputees

In the U.S., health care professionals determine a lower limb amputee's level of functioning/limitations by using a ranking system known as K-levels. The K-level system classifies amputees into five distinct classes. Code modifiers (K0, K1, K2, K3, and K4) are used to categorize functional abilities. The lower the amputee's potential for activity, the lower their amputee K-level.

An amputee's K-level is considered dynamic and could change over time, in one direction or the other. For example, a motivated amputee would likely go up in K-levels. Health insurance plans determine a lower limb amputee's eligibility for a prosthetic leg, and associated components, based on the patient's individual K-level. After a K-level is assigned, the class of prosthetic is determined and the amputee can purchase it. The following is the K-level ranking system:

- **K0:** No Level of Mobility. The amputee does not have the ability and/or potential to transfer or ambulate safely with or without assistance. A prosthetic device will not enhance the mobility and/or quality of life.

- **K1:** Very Limited Level of Mobility. This type of amputee has the ability and/or potential to use prosthesis for ambulation and/or transfers on level surfaces at a fixed walking speed rather than walking at a variable pace and/or bypassing any kind of obstacles.

- **K2:** Limited Level of Mobility. This lower limb amputee possesses the ability and/or potential to utilize prosthesis for ambulation as well as the ability to adjust for low-level barriers including stairs, curbs and/or uneven surfaces. This level of amputee may walk for limited time period but cannot vary their speed significantly.

- **K3:** Basic to Normal Level of Mobility. The amputee has the ability and/or potential to use their prosthesis for basic ambulation as well as the ability to adjust for the majority of environmental barriers. They also have the ability to walk at various speeds.

- **K4:** High Level of Activity. Exceeding basic mobility levels, a K4 amputee applies high impact and stress to their prosthetic device. Typically, this would include amputees such as children, active adults and/or athletes.

Stroke Patients

In 1998, the American Heart Association developed a valid, reliable global classification system that summarizes the neurological impairments, disabilities, and handicaps that take place following a stroke. A stroke outcome classification system assumes that neurological deficits often result in permanent disabilities and impairments as well as a compromised quality of life. While a stroke patient's ability to complete various functional, everyday tasks is primarily thought to be dependent on and generally limited by the degree and type of impairment, other factors can be relevant in the ultimate functional outcome determination.

Therefore, a stroke outcome classification should include broad ranges of impairments and disabilities, as well as the relationship of impairment and disability to independent functioning. Many factors determine a stroke patient's level of functioning, including the influences of both a post-stroke rehabilitation program and physical and social environments.

The AHA Stroke Outcome Classification (AHA.SOC) score classifies the extent and severity of neurological impairments, which are considered to be the basis for disability. In addition, this classification system identifies the independence level of stroke patients according to basic and more complex activities of daily living within the patient's home and within their community.

Stroke Outcome Classification

AHA.SOC Score: _____ · _____ · _____

     # Domains Severity Function

Neurological Domains = Motor, vision, cognition, language, affect, sensory

Number of Neurological Domains Impaired:

Score:

- 0 = 0 domains impaired.

- 1 = 1 domains impaired.

- 2 = 2 domains impaired.

- 3 ≥ 2 domains impaired.

Impairment Severity:

- Level A: No to minimal neurological deficit due to stroke within any domain.

- Level B: Mild to moderate deficit resulting from stroke in ≥ 1 domain(s).

- Level C: Severe deficit resulting from stroke in ≥ 1 domain(s).

Levels of Function:

- Level I: Independent - in Basic Activities of Daily Living (BADL) and Instrumental Activities of Daily Living (IADL), i.e., the tasks and/or activities the patient had prior to stroke. At this level, the patient can live alone, take care of a household, access local community for leisure activities as well as shopping, employment, etc.

- Level II: Independent - in BADL but partially dependent in routine IADL. Stroke patient is capable of living alone but needs help or supervision to access their local community. May occasionally need help with preparing meals, taking medications and/or completing household jobs

- Level III: Partially Dependent - in BADL (< 3 areas) and IADL. This person is capable of living independently with substantial daily help from family and/or community resources for more difficult BADL (e.g. dressing, bathing, climbing stairs, etc.). Needs help with preparing meals, taking medications, handling personal finances, completing household maintenance, shopping and/or accessing their local community

- Level IV: Partially Dependent - in BADL (≥ 3 areas). Stroke patient is not capable of living alone safely. Also requires assistance with IADL with the exception of simple tasks (e.g. answering the telephone)

- Level V: Completely Dependent - in BADL (≥ 5 areas) and IADL. Individual is incapable of living on their own safely. Needs care on a full-time basis

- BADL = feeding, swallowing, dressing, grooming, bathing, toileting, continence and mobility

- IADL = shopping, handling money, using the telephone, using public transportation, maintaining a home, working, taking part in leisure activities

Patient Education and Goals of the Cardiac/Vascular Education Plan

The overarching goal of any focused cardiac/vascular education plan, including cardiac rehabilitation and cardiac/vascular patient education, is to increase the patient's chances of survival. Other goals include:

- Assisting the patient to regain strength

- Preventing their cardiac/vascular condition(s) from becoming any worse

- Reducing the risks of future heart problems

- Properly educating the patient concerning their own condition(s), self-care, maintenance program, lifestyle changes, etc.

- Development of positive behaviors

- Improving the cardiac vascular patient's overall quality of life

Self-Care Strategies

Successful management of cardiac/vascular conditions requires compliance on the part of the patient, family and/or caregivers. In turn, compliance requires appropriate education. Before appropriate education can be given, assessment of the patient's needs, goals, beliefs, standards of judgment, and skills comprehension must be ascertained.

Considerations for Adult Learners

- Create a collaborative environment
- Determine the patient's preferred way of learning, such as visual, auditory, and/or kinesthetic.
- Understand that the patient brings their own personal experiences to education sessions
- Understand that social roles play a part in the learning process
- Explain that immediate application of learned information will increase the likelihood for behavioral changes

Learning Needs of the Cardiac/Vascular Patient

- Determine the levels of motivation of the patient, family, and caregivers
- Ascertain what factors motivate behavioral changes on behalf of the CV patient
- Ascertain their existing base of knowledge for various CV topics
- Determine their previous experiences with specific CV conditions/diseases
- Enquire whether particular cultural issues may play a part in adapting to new behaviors
- Assess the literacy level of the patient and/or members of their support system
- Determine the availability of educational materials on particular CV topics.
- Identify if there are any learning barriers, such as poor writing/reading skills, time commitment, lack of persistence/motivation, gender discrimination, age, language/speech/hearing/mobility/cognitive issues, pain, fatigue, depression, and/or lack of support

- Determine how educational attainment and/or behavioral changes will be evaluated (ANCC, 2014)

Appropriate Presentation Styles

Type of Learner	Learning Characteristics	Sample Approaches
Visual	Diagrams, pictures, and/or other visuals	Lots of visual props (e.g. PowerPoint slides, booklets, diagrams and trigger cards)
Auditory	Verbal instructions, may find visuals distracting	Oral descriptions, lectures, podcasts, audio CDs, DVDs, etc.
Kinesthetic (i.e. using parts of the body)	Movement and "hands-on" types of activities	Physical demonstrations, simulations, role playing and group discussions

Implementation and Evaluation

To effectively implement and evaluate a focused cardiac/vascular education plan, the CV nurse must have knowledge of techniques involved in teaching patients and their loved ones. This involves group dynamics, conflict resolution, and how to measure attainment of the education plan goals. In addition, he or she must possess skills in organizing necessary information and instructional activities related to weight management, smoking cessation, physical activity, health maintenance, and/or promotion.

A CV nurse must also have the necessary skills to effectively deliver presentations such as lectures, discussions, return demonstrations, coaching, and counseling. Lastly, evaluation and possible revision of the educational program, in terms of clarity, accuracy, and attainment of goals, is required upon completion.

Individual/Group Teaching Techniques

Adult learners can be challenging to teach/educate based on certain needs, considerations and/or barriers to their learning, as listed earlier. The following chart briefly describes individual learning and different sized group learning environments.

Group Size	Characteristics	Advantages/Disadvantages
Individual	• Promotes personal reflections • Generates personal data	• Focus on one person increases individual's perception of safety • Individual focus generally means a positive beginning to the educational session. • Person brings a sense of ownership and/or belonging to the session.
Two to Three	• Generating and checking out data • Sharing of interpretations of information • Good for skills practice and basic communication (e.g. questioning, listening and/or clarifying) • Ideal size for co-operative working and learning	• Builds perceptions of safety • Builds levels of confidence by actively involving group members (i.e. promotes sense of self-belief) • Lays the foundation for co-operation and/or sharing of information in bigger group settings • Reticent/shy members can still participate effectively

Four to Ten	• Generation of ideas • Criticism of ideas • Generally adequate numbers to allow for defined responsibilities and/or roles • Wide range of activities can be implemented (e.g. problem-based learning, group exercises, etc.)	• Decreasing levels of safety for shy/reticent members • At lower end of the size range, still difficult for individual members to 'hide' but this possibility increases as the size of the group increases • Strong members can still encourage weaker members • Size of group still small enough for instructor to maintain overall control • Sufficient resources to allow for creative support
Eleven or More	• Maintaining focused learning becomes somewhat more challenging • Group size can hinder effective discussion but makes workshop activities possible (e.g. using effective sub-groups to address issues)	• More difficulty in maintaining a supportive environment • 'Hiding' becomes more common • Temptation for individual group members to dominate • Struggles in leadership become a risk • Possibilities for divisive behaviour and spontaneous division into sub-groups

Group Dynamics and Conflict Resolution

It is also important to consider group dynamics and processes as well as the possible need for conflict resolution. The following is an example of a multi-level framework that describes the various characteristics of group learning which includes "forming", "norming", "storming", "performing", "adjourning" and "mourning."

1. Forming: When a group "forms," the members are first coming together. The instructor can assist in getting things started by facilitating proper introductions of group members, using "ice-breaking" activities, as well as explaining the overall purpose, tasks, and ultimate goals of the group.

2. Norming: In this stage, group members and the facilitator/teacher start to share ideas, thoughts and beliefs with each other. They also develop shared norms as well as establish rules for group interactions. It is the responsibility of the teacher to help clarify ideas and/or ground rules, encourage quieter and/or shy patients to participate and move the group along towards its defined purpose.

3. Storming: During the "storming" stage, the group is actively attempting to complete a set task. At this point, there may be a certain amount of conflict between two or more members as the dynamics of the group solidify. However, it actually becomes more functional in the process. The teacher/facilitator will find it useful to clarify/reflect on key concepts and ideas, smooth over and moderate any conflicts as well as act as a "go-between" among members.

4. Performing: This is a very important stage. "Performing" is when the group concentrates on the assigned activity and begins to effectively work together as a team in order to accomplish the set goals. The teacher should ensure that the group remains focused, encouraging and facilitating, when appropriate.

5. Adjourning/Mourning: When a group has successfully worked together, the final stage(s) can be referred to as "adjourning" and/or "mourning". A well-functioning group looks back on its achievements, and the contributions of individual group members. It reflects on lessons learned, aspects that seemed to work effectively as well as those things that could have worked better.

Sometimes, a group can revert back into the "norming" and/or "storming" stages. Often, this will occur when there are personality clashes within the group, problems with learning and/or understanding of specific tasks/concepts. A good teacher needs to closely watch the group process, tasks, and outputs, and he or she must intervene if needed. A democratic discussion group involves having the leader make the right kinds of interventions. This particular role can be much less demanding and/or stressful by utilizing more structure in proceedings and less intervention in group processes.

Measuring Goal Attainment

The majority of cardiac rehabilitation programs and other CV disease prevention programs include multidisciplinary interventions that focus on the reduction of risk factors as well as the promotion of a healthy lifestyle.

A specific measurement tool which accurately assesses a cardiac/vascular patient's knowledge, both before and after taking an educational program, needs to be included within clinical settings. Normally, cardiac rehabilitation professionals utilize a self-administered patient questionnaire, known as the Maugeri Cardiac Prevention Questionnaire (it is shortened to MICRO-Q in a somewhat counterintuitive way: **M**auger**I** **CaR**diac preventi**O**n **Q**uestionnaire.) The MICRO-Q consists of 26 statements where 18 of the statements are true and the other eight are false. These statements include knowledge of risk factors, diet, lifestyle, pre-admission avoidable delays as well as cardiac disease knowledge. A patient responds to these statements with "true", "false", or "don't know".

Three separate MICRO-Q scores are provided:

- Correct: The number of correctly answered items

- Misconceptions: The number of incorrectly answered

- Uncertainty: The number of items answered with "don't know,"

Information and Instructional Activities

A cardiac/vascular nurse should have skill in organizing informational handouts as well as CV instructional activities.

Weight Management

Maintaining a healthy weight is very important for cardiac/vascular patients. Being overweight or obese puts them at a much higher risk of cardiac/vascular problems and other diseases such as diabetes, cancer, etc. Having a healthy body weight can aid in the control of blood pressure, cholesterol and/or blood sugar levels. A weight-control or weight maintenance strategy typically includes:

- Choosing low-fat, low-calorie, low-sugar, and/or low-sodium foods

- Eating smaller meal portions

- Drinking lots of water rather than sugary drinks like juices and/or sodas

- Being physically active

Smoking Cessation

Cardiac/vascular patients who smoke should be strongly advised to stop immediately, as smoking is a major risk factor for both heart disease and lung cancer. Smoking cessation can be very difficult, and patients need to be encouraged to get "started at stopping" for the sake of their overall health. The smoking cessation strategy known as **START** incudes:

- **S = Setting a firm date to quit:** A C/V patient should pick a quitting date within the next two weeks, so they have ample time to prepare without losing the motivation to stop smoking.

- **T = Tell family, friends and co-workers:** Informing family and friends will allow them to give their encouragement and support in a smoking cessation plan. Finding a "quit buddy" who wants to stop smoking can also be beneficial.

- **A = Anticipate/plan for facing challenges along the way:** Preparing ahead of time for common smoking challenges, including nicotine withdrawal and cigarette cravings, is important.

- **R = Remove tobacco products from home, work and vehicles:** Throw away all cigarettes, lighters, matches and ashtrays. Freshen up anything that smells of smoke such as clothing, drapes, carpets, furniture and/or vehicles.

- **T = Talk to professionals about getting help to quit:** Doctors can prescribe medications to help with nicotine withdrawal as well as suggest other alternatives. These include nicotine patches, lozenges and/or gum.

Physical Activity Guidelines

Physical activity is essential for cardiac/vascular patients. According to the American Heart Association, individuals who need to lower their blood pressure and/or cholesterol levels should undertake 40 minutes of aerobic exercise, at moderate to vigorous intensity. This should be done three to four times per week, in order to reduce their risks for heart attack and/or stroke.

Examples of physical activity that benefit the heart include aerobic exercise such as jogging, walking, biking, and swimming. By comparison, strength and stretching is beneficial for overall flexibility and stamina. Cardiac/vascular patients need to make some form of physical activity a regular, satisfying part of their everyday life.

Overall Cardiovascular Health:

- Minimum of 30 minutes of moderate intensity aerobic type exercise, at least 5 days weekly, for a total of 150 minutes or:

- Minimum of 25 minutes of vigorous aerobic exercise, at least 3 days weekly, for a total of 75 minutes; or a combination of moderate-intensity and vigorous-intensity aerobic activity <u>and</u>:

- Moderate to high intensity muscle strengthening exercises for a minimum of 2 days a week for additional health benefits

To Lower Blood Pressure and Cholesterol:

Average of 40 minutes of moderate to vigorous intensity aerobic type activity 3 to 4 times weekly.

Health Maintenance/Promotion

Practicing healthy life habits can lower the risks of the harmful effects of stress and other medical conditions including cardiac/vascular conditions, depression, and other disorders. The following is a list of 10 positive health habits that all cardiac/vascular patients should be encouraged to adopt in order to maintain and/or improve their overall health:

- Talk with family/friends.

- Engage in daily physical activity.

- Accept the things you cannot change.

- Laugh.

- Give up bad habits.

- Slow down.

- Get plenty of sleep.

- Organize your life.

- Practice giving back to others.

- Try to stop worrying (AHA, 2014).

Effective Presentations

A cardiac/vascular nurse should have the necessary skills to deliver effective presentations to their patients in order to help them learn about the various aspects of their CV condition and any related medical care. Regardless of the type of presentation, effective delivery techniques include:

- Establishing and maintaining eye contact with patients

- Using gestures and physical movements that complement verbal statements, as with looking directly at patients when asking for questions or answers

- Practicing the use of any accompanying audiovisual aids in advance

- Avoiding the use of distracting physical movements and/or gestures, such as grooming and pacing

Lectures

The term "lecturing" refers to the planning and delivering of a presentation within a classroom setting. While a lecture has some common components with a formal speech, a lecture places more emphasis on instructor-student interactions. Below is a list of suggestions for effective preparation and delivery of a lecture. The lecture should be divided into the three main parts - introduction, body and conclusion:

Introduction

- Plan an introduction that will capture an audience's interest

- Give a brief overview of the lecture's content

- Inform patients what you expect them to do with the lecture material

- Explain/define all unfamiliar and/or technical terminology

Body

- Make sure to be well organized beforehand

- Logically organize material

- Build enough time into the lecture for summarizing of key points as well as allowing for relevant examples to illustrate/support key points

- Ask for, and thoroughly answer, all patients' questions. Get back to them as soon as possible, if unsure of an answer

<u>Conclusion</u>

- Answer any questions raised, at the beginning and/or during the course of the lecture.

- Provide proper closure for the lecture.

- Restate expectations of the ongoing use of lecture information

Effective Discussions

A cardiac/vascular discussion leader assists group members in their understanding, appreciation and/or evaluation of the educational material being presented. This is accomplished by facilitating a relevant conversation. A brief agenda will help the group stay on track. Below are some suggested elements of a discussion agenda:

1. A quick "check-in" period. Allow each member of the group to speak briefly. They can introduce themselves and mention anything that is relevant to the topic.

2. State the discussion's objectives. Briefly give any required background and/or orientation to the topic. Distribute any handouts.

3. Pick a patient to keep notes of the group's ideas. Provide appropriate writing materials.

4. Get the discussion started. Guide it, keep it moving and on track. Attempt to get all members involved. It can be beneficial to write out key points and questions you plan to ask. Arrange them in logical order. The questions should stimulate thinking and group discussion.

5. As the discussion nears its end, summarize the main points that were covered. Clarify anything that patients either found confusing or did not understand. Allow participants to ask any final questions.

6. Conduct a brief "check-out." Give group members an opportunity to evaluate the quality of the discussed material

Return Demonstration

The return demonstration method of instruction shows cardiac/vascular patients how to do a specified task by utilizing sequential instructions. The ultimate goal is to have patients perform the assigned task on their own. Demonstrations can be used by a C/V nurse to enhance classroom lectures/discussions with hands-on, inquiry-based learning as well as within one-on-one settings.

When using the return demonstration model, the instructor performs the task in a step-by-step fashion so that students will eventually be able to independently complete the same task. Eventually, patients should be able to not just duplicate the task but also be able to figure out how to problem-solve, if unexpected problems and/or obstacles arise. At this point, the instructor's role is to support students in their ongoing attempts. The cardiac/vascular nurse provides guidance, feedback, and suggestions for alternate approaches.

Coaching

The cardiac/vascular nurse "coach" utilizes active listening, powerful questioning and direct communication to help patients with the identification of goals, development of action steps and evaluation of their progress. Patient coaching is typically used to teach patients and to facilitate their ongoing adherence to self-care practices related to chronic cardiac/vascular conditions such as heart failure. Effective coaching allows for excellent communication with patients, families and/or caregivers. This promotes collaborative practice and support of behavioral changes.

Benefits of patient coaching can include the following:

- Easing the burden on family members and/or caregivers

- Enhancing patients' and caregivers' confidence related to medical care

- Properly preparing patients to complete cardiac/vascular disease self-care

Patient coaching stages:

- Stage I (Assessment stage): CV nurse/coach establishes the relationship and identifies the patient's readiness to change.

- Stage II: Nurse/coach helps patients remember that they are the ultimate authority in their life. Thus, they hold the right solutions to changing/improving their lifestyle.

- Stage III: Nurse/coach makes use of powerful questioning to help patients identify their opportunities, concerns, and desired/expected outcomes.

- Stage IV (Planning stage): Nurse/coach helps the patient make a plan as well as challenges them in positive ways.

- Stage V (Implementation stage): Focuses on motivating and empowering patients to effect positive lifestyle changes.

Counseling

The definition of counseling is to give advice and support to an individual in order to help them deal with various life problems, such as physical, social, psychological, mental issues, and to make important life-changing decisions associated with these problems. Modifications to cardiac risk factors as well as lifestyle changes are essential to the success of any cardiac rehabilitation program. Ultimately, program goals are to limit the physiological effects of cardiac/vascular disease as well as to improve the patient's overall fitness and health.

In addition to patient education and prescribed exercise training, counseling is another important component of a comprehensive cardiac rehab program. Since cardiac/vascular nurses are important members of the interdisciplinary team, they can provide valuable counseling to cardiac/vascular patients. This involves giving constant advice and support to patients, family members and/or caregivers.

The vast majority of cardiac/vascular patients and their family members experience uncertainties including the fear of having another C/V event, coping with changes in lifestyle, worrying about hospital bills and/or what the future will hold for them. The knowledge that there is a team available to guide them through their recovery has been proven to be both effective and beneficial.

Evaluation/Revision

After a cardiac/vascular educational program has been completed by a patient, it is essential that the focused program be evaluated and revised, if necessary. Depending on the particular facility, this may be one of the cardiac/vascular nurse's responsibilities. Utilizing the MICRO-Q patient questionnaire mentioned above, the CV patient should be questioned concerning the program's overall clarity, accuracy, and effectiveness concerning their goal attainment expectations.

Professional Role Performance (27%)

The Nurse-Patient Relationship

One of the most important responsibilities of a professional cardiac/vascular nurse is the establishment and maintenance of a therapeutic nurse-patient relationship. They need to have knowledge of crisis counseling for patients and families during cardiac/vascular emergencies. CV nurses need to be aware of certain coping/defense mechanisms that may be used by patients when they experience cardiac/vascular events.

Skills are needed in establishing and maintaining therapeutic relationships with a patient's family members, significant others and/or caregivers. This includes taking into account grief and loss, family dynamics, cultural diversity, and aspects of conflict resolution.

Crisis Counseling for Patients/Families during Cardiac/Vascular Emergencies

Research studies have shown that using various interventions actually reduce cardiovascular events and related deaths by at least 50%. Coronary heart disease is not just a physical condition; it also has a significant psychological component.

Rather than just using biomedical therapies during an emergency cardiac/vascular event (heart attack, acute heart failure, etc.), there is also a great deal of benefit in providing crisis counseling, including certain psychological interventions. Doing so can ease immediate anxiety and stress in patients and their family/caregivers at the time of an event. However, it can also reduce the chances of patients dying or having repeat cardiovascular events with fewer associated hospital visits.

Interventions

Crisis counseling interventions may include the following:

- Taking the extra time to quietly talk to patients and their families about their current and ongoing worries and issues
- Showing them how to do relaxation and visualization exercises.
- Playing quiet, relaxing music
- Saying prayers with religious patients and finding the hospital chaplain to provide spiritual support

Coping and Defense Mechanisms during Cardiac/Vascular Events

Denial can be defined as a psychological coping strategy, or basic defense mechanism, that enables individuals to engage in certain risky types of behavior with little or no conscious awareness of the consequences. For example, patients can deny the existence of a newly diagnosed heart disease. They can refuse to modify various CV risk factors that they have control over, including reducing hypertension, increasing exercise levels, stopping smoking, and losing weight.

Studies have shown that using denial has long-term detrimental effects on cardiovascular disease outcomes and at certain critical points in time, such as during an acute cardiovascular event. One of the greatest dangers is that denial can contribute to negative cardiovascular outcomes. Patients may deny that a cardiac event is occurring. Denial is actually one of the first coping mechanisms that patients use during highly stressful events like acute chest pain episodes.

It has yet to be determined if denial, used to reduce levels of fear, anxiety, and other unpleasant emotions, directly results in greater delays in seeking medical assistance during acute cardiac events. Individuals that delay getting medical treatment are at greater risk for myocardial damage, burden of disease, and death. In addition, it is thought that extended denial of negative emotions and/or problems may significantly increase the risks of developing coronary heart disease.

Therapeutic Relationship with CV Patients, Families and/or Caregivers

A positive, therapeutic nurse/patient relationship occurs when a cardiac/vascular nurse promotes a sense of mutual trust and encourages the patient to express their feelings and/or thoughts. The nurse treats the patient as a person, not just a diagnosis.

Types of Communication

The nurse can utilize many different types of therapeutic communication that indicate a sense of caring, sincerity, empathy and trustworthiness to patients. Therapeutic communication also benefits their physical and mental states. Types of therapeutic communication include verbal (closed questioning, open-ended questioning and restating), non-verbal (active and passive), listening, silence, touch, and humor.

Verbal

Verbal communication involves communicating with the use of spoken words and/or symbols. This includes:

- Closed Questioning – Focuses on seeking a specific answer
- Open-ended Questioning – Does not need a specific answer, which allows patients to elaborate freely
- Re-stating – Repeating to the patient what the nurse understands to be their main point

Non-Verbal

Non-verbal communication involves communicating without the use of words and body language. It still conveys listening, interest, and caring. This includes:

- Active – Listening and giving full attention to speaker.
- Passive – No feedback, but communication is accomplished via eye contact and/or nodding.

Listening

- Most effective skill to acquire but most difficult to acquire
- Shows caring and interest

Silence

- Most unused communication technique
- Needs timing and skill to perfect the appropriate amount of silence to use

Touch

- Must be used with a great deal of discretion
- Conveys warmth, support, caring and understanding
- Must be genuine, otherwise it can be construed as rejection
- The appropriateness of touch is highly dependent on cultural considerations

Humor

- The "best medicine," but use with caution
- Provides physical and psychological release
- Enhances sense of well-being
- Reduces anxiety
- Effective in increasing patient's pain threshold
- Only appropriate to laugh WITH a patient, not AT them

Factors that affect Communication

- Environment – should be calm and relaxed
- Trust – essential for a therapeutic nurse/patient relationship
- Language Barriers – try keeping communication simple, acting things out and/or getting a translator
- Culture/Religion – awareness of differences when caring for patients
- Age and Gender – some older patients do not trust younger healthcare professionals. In some cultures, patients prefer medical care by same sex (e.g. Muslims)
- Physiological – extreme pain, altered cognition, etc. can be barriers
- Psychological – stress can be a barrier

Establishing Rapport with Patient

- Be reliable
- Listen to the patient
- Anticipate needs
- Educate the patient, as required
- Stay in control, and give patient a small amount of control as well
- Show support with small gestures

- Treat patient as an individual
- Use humor appropriately
- Make use of self-disclosure, such as intentional sharing of personal information

Grief and Loss

The stages of grief, mourning and loss are considered to be universal. Mourning can occur in response to an individual's own terminal illness. It can also occur as a result of the terminal illness and/or death of a valued friend, family member and/or loved one. There are five different stages of grief and loss which a person might experience. Stages can occur in any order and/or may not happen at all. They include:

1. Denial and isolation
2. Anger
3. Bargaining
4. Depression
5. Acceptance

Family Dynamics

Family dynamics are varying interactions occurring between family members as well as the many relationships that can exist within any family. All families have some kind of dynamics. Three important components of family dynamics include:

- Inherited patterns of relating to one another
- Assigned roles
- Invisible, unwritten rules

These processes inform each family member how they should act, how they should respond to others and what is expected of them. Within every family, dynamics have good aspects (healthy) and bad aspects (pathological) which tend to determine a member's general sense of health, happiness, and/or stability. As medical professionals, cardiac/vascular nurses should possess skills in identifying, respecting and being sensitive to their patients' unique family dynamics regardless of culture and/or ethnicity.

Culture and Diversity

Within the US, there are many diverse ethic and/or racial groups. As part of establishing and maintaining positive therapeutic relationships with their patients, cardiac/vascular nurses should never assume that their patients belong to a particular group. A racial group is defined as those who share certain biological/physical traits, such as skin color, hair color, and eye color. On the other hand, members of an ethnic group identify with each other by presumed common genealogy, ancestry, cultural/religious beliefs and/or traditions, etc. Often, people belong to more than one culture.

When developing a CV patient care plan, it is important to assess the patient's culture and/or behaviors, and act accordingly. It should be noted that not all members of a particular ethnic group necessarily exhibit the same types of behaviors because of different geographical locations, gender roles, individuality and other factors. Always avoid stereotyping.

However, there are general guidelines one can follow when caring for an individual of a certain culture until the nurse gets to know the individual well. For example, the following is a list of various cultural aspects that should be both respected and taken into consideration when caring for patients with Mexican heritage:

- May believe in biomedical and folk healers, as well as rituals and health care models
- May speak both Spanish and English
- Touch frequently but always ask permission first
- Patients may be modest
- Family expects to help with care, and members take turns around the clock
- Typically, males are consulted about health care decisions
- Only the wife touches a male patient's genitals
- Small children are shielded from death
- Lactose intolerance is common

Resolving Conflict

It is imperative for nurses to remember that the foundation of nursing care is the positive therapeutic nurse/patient relationship, which directly contributes to the patient's overall well-being and health. This therapeutic relationship can become threatened whenever there is the possibility of conflict between the nurse and the patient, their family members, friends, caregivers and/or other medical colleagues. Conflict can negatively impact communication, collaboration and/or teamwork.

Nurses also need to keep in mind that they share responsibility with their employers in the creation of a healthy workplace environment, which ensures that conflict does not impede patients' health outcomes and/or professional relationships amongst colleagues. By fostering collaborative, mutually agreeable solutions, nurses can decrease, if not totally eliminate, conflict. This can be accomplished by using good communication skills and helping to facilitate conflict resolution between individuals.

Patient Safety and Quality

In any patient care setting, patient safety and high quality of care are key components of the facility's mission statement. As a result, it is essential that cardiac/vascular nurses have knowledge of infection control and prevention, including sub-acute bacterial endocarditis prophylaxis. In addition, they should have skills in managing patient risk, associated with cardiac/vascular diagnoses and procedures, and skills in the gathering, analyzing and the use of data trends to identify areas for improvement.

Infection Prevention

Every year, deaths occur in hospital settings as a result of the spread of infections. All health care workers can help eliminate risks by practicing effective infection control. The single most effective method of stopping the spread of germs and associated infections is the use of frequent, proper hand washing techniques. Other steps health care workers can take include:

- Coughing and/or sneezing into the sleeves, NOT the hands
- Keeping all immunizations up-to-date
- Using gloves, masks and protective clothing
- Making tissues and hand cleaners available for all staff and visitors to use
- Following institutional guidelines concerning the handling of blood products and/or contaminated items

Sub-Acute Bacterial Endocarditis Prophylaxis

Endocarditis is an infection of the heart's endocardium, valves and/or cardiac prosthesis resulting from an invasion of either bacteria or fungus. Fibrin and platelets cluster on valve tissues engulfing the circulating bacteria or fungus. This process produces vegetation that can cover the surfaces of the valves, leading to deformities and/or destruction of the valve tissues. Endocarditis can also lead to valvular insufficiency. Untreated endocarditis is typically fatal. However, 70% of patients recover when properly treated. The prognosis worsens if there is severe damage to the heart valves.

Patients with certain cardiac conditions (e.g. congenital heart diseases and malformations) are predisposed to endocarditis. Thus they are at an increased risk for bacterial endocarditis when they undergo open heart surgeries. Cardiac/vascular patients who have prosthetic heart valve placement procedures, prosthetic intravascular placements or intra-cardiac material placement surgeries are at an increased risk for bacterial endocarditis. Therefore, prophylactic antibiotics are recommended during surgery. The incidence of bacterial endocarditis following the majority of procedures is quite low in C/V patients with underlying cardiac disease(s). According to the AHA, a reasonable approach to endocarditis prophylaxis should consider these factors:

- Degree that the patient's underlying condition creates endocarditis risk
- Apparent risk of bacteremia during the procedure
- Possible adverse effects of the prophylactic agent being used
- Overall cost-benefit ratio of the recommended prophylactic antibiotic regiment

Managing Patient Risk

Risk management is defined as an organization-wide service that identifies and takes actions to reduce the danger of patient loss and/or harm. Programs of risk management can include:

- Identification of potential hazards
- Review of monitoring systems
- Analysis and/or categorization of incidents
- Review and tracking of laws
- Elimination of risk
- Identification of educational/training needs
- Preparation of administrative reports

Gathering, Analyzing, and Using Data Trends

Quality indicators (QIs) were developed by the Agency for Healthcare Research and Quality (AHRQ), and are a response to the need for accessible, multidimensional quality measures that can be used to gauge health care performance. QIs are evidence based and can be utilized to identify variations in the quality of care given on an inpatient and outpatient basis. Currently organized into four modules, these measures are:

- Prevention Quality Indicators (PQIs): Identify ambulatory care sensitive conditions (i.e. conditions where good outpatient care can possibly prevent the need for hospitalization and/or early intervention may prevent complications or the development of more severe disease.)

- Inpatient Quality Indicators (IQIs): Reflect quality of care inside hospitals including inpatient mortality, utilization of procedures where there are questions of overuse, underuse and/or misuse, as well as procedure volumes where there is evidence that a higher volume of procedures relates to lower patient mortality.

- Patient Safety Indicators (PSIs): Focus on preventable complication instances and other medical treatment events resulting from health care system exposure.

- Pediatric Quality Indicators (PDIs): Reflect quality of care for children under 17 years of age and newborns inside hospitals (i.e. provider-level indicators). These QIs identify possible avoidable hospitalizations among children (i.e. area-level indicators).

Nurses are integral health care team members in a unique position to detect quality of care issues, often paving the way for change in improvements in the quality and safety of health care processes. AHRQ QIs are performance measures that provide quality of care information. Nurses can utilize them in planning and implementing quality improvement strategies.

Data obtained from the AHRQ QIs can be used to effectively track trends, identify data measurement gaps and assist in redesigning organizational/workflow processes. Gathered data provide a focus for improving health care quality. It can be used to make informed decisions concerning facility, community and/or regional policies. Nurses are well-positioned to review performance data, interpret results, provide additional follow-up and design interventions to improve organizational quality of care

Patient Rights (Legal and Ethical)

Any patient has the right to:

- Receive considerate and respectful care
- Receive enough information to make informed consent
- Receive information about care alternatives
- Refuse (treatments)
- Privacy
- Confidential communication
- Expect a hospital to make a reasonable response to their request for service
- Be informed about human experimentation
- Expect reasonable continuity of care
- Receive/examine an explanation of a hospital invoice
- Know a hospital's rules/regulations

Cardiac/Vascular Nursing Regulations and Standards of Care

A CV nurse must have knowledge of the regulations and standards of care associated with cardiac/vascular nursing as well as the necessary skills to advocate for their cardiac/vascular patients. The American Nursing Association (ANA) is the professional organization that represents all registered nurses within the United State. As defined by the ANA, nursing ethics refers to the standards of moral behaviors (and how nurses respond to them) that take place within nursing practice.

ANA Code for Nurses

The American Nurses Association (ANA) *Code for Nurses with Interpretive Statements* (Code for Nurses) explicates the goals, values, and ethical precepts that direct the profession of nursing. The ANA believes the *Code for Nurses* is nonnegotiable and that each nurse has an obligation to uphold and adhere to the code of ethics (ANA, 2014).

Certifying and Regulating Bodies

- ANCC – The American Nurses Credentialing Center (ANCC) is an affiliate of the ANA that conducts certification examinations as well as certifies advanced practice nurses.
- Board – The State Board of Nursing is the appointed body responsible for the administration of the Nursing Practice Act within each state.

The Nursing Practice Acts (NPAs)

The Nursing Practice Acts are the statutes that establish the legal regulations (i.e. laws) that govern the scope of nursing practice (activities nurses can perform legally) within each state and territory. The components of these Acts include:

- Purposes of Act
- Protection of the health and safety of citizens
- Definition of nursing and scope of practice
- Licensure requirements
- Renewal of licensure
- Mandatory continuing education
- Sunset legislation, which includes statutes that provide for law revocation if not reviewed and renewed within a specified time
- Makes sure legislation is current and reflects the public's needs
- Ensures NPA is reviewed by a certain date, and if not, it is automatically rescinded

Nursing Journals

Some examples of nursing research journals include the American Journal of Nursing, which is the oldest, most honored, broad-based nursing journal worldwide. Peer-reviewed and evidence-based, it is considered to be the nursing profession's premier journal. The mission of this journal is to promote nursing and health care excellence by:

- Dissemination of clinical information and original research content.
- Discussion of relevant as well as controversial professional nursing issues.
- Adherence to the standards of journalistic integrity/excellence.
- Promotion of nursing perspectives to the health care community and public

Advocacy

Advocacy is defined as expressing and defending the interests of those (cardiac/vascular patients) who are unable to speak for themselves. They may include elderly patients who have no family members and/or patients who have communication issues. As well as pleading a patient's case, a CV nurse can act as a patient advocate by respecting the patient's independence. Additionally, nurse advocates ensure that the patient receives complete access to appropriate levels of medical, mental, and spiritual healthcare based on their particular cardiac/vascular disease/disorder and other co-existing condition(s).

Leadership Roles

Cardiac/vascular nurses need to have knowledge of leadership roles, including being mentors, preceptors, context experts, and the shared governance model in nursing. They must also know about various communication strategies and methods as they pertain to cardiac/vascular nursing. In addition, cardiac/vascular nurses must develop skills in the appropriate delegation of responsibilities as well as skills in establishing and maintaining communication among members of the interdisciplinary team.

Mentors

A mentor is defined as an experienced, trusted adviser who acts as a coach, advisor, friend, cheerleader, and counselor to another colleague. Nurse mentors can accomplish the following for their protégés:

- Help open doors to new learning and career opportunities

- Expose them to different viewpoints concerning their professional work and the many challenges they face

- Push them outside of their comfort zones

- Assist with building protégés' self-awareness as nursing professionals

- Provide gentle, constructive feedback on specific behaviors that may be hindering progress of their nursing careers

- Act as a trusted sounding board for their thoughts and ideas

- Help them grow as individuals

Mentors do not evaluate their protégés, nor do they have any direct links to protégés' supervisors. Mentor-protégé relationships are empowering for both parties. They are non-competitive, non-judgemental, and built on mutual trust and respect. In difficult times, nurse mentors celebrate their protégés' successes and give them much needed support.

Preceptors

Unlike mentors, trained preceptors are paired with newly hired nurses and play active roles in the orientation process to the new clinical setting. Preceptors act as educators, role models, socializers, friends, and confidantes. The formal portion of the relationship between the preceptor and newly hired staff member generally ends at the conclusion of the orientation period. The major roles of preceptors include the following:

- Explain a particular facility's policies and procedures.
- Teach unfamiliar nursing skills to the new hire.
- Help the new nurse perform these newly learned skills.
- Observe the new nurse complete these skills, without any assistance.
- Evaluate the new hire's progress and/or competencies

Content Experts

Content experts can play a major leadership role in the largest, most prestigious national credentialing body for nurses known as the American Nurses Credentialing Center (ANCC). The ANCC looks for content experts for all of its certification and assessment based certificate programs. A nursing content expert can perform the following functions:

- Item writer and collaborator on the development and/or updating of test content
- Active member on standards setting panels to establish passing scores

<u>Benefits of Being a Nursing Content Expert</u>

- Playing a dynamic role in developing your specific area of nursing expertise and/or subject matter expertise.
- Enhancing your curriculum vitae (CV).

- Collaborating with other nursing colleagues across the country.

- Earning a reduction in the number of contact hours needed to renew ANCC certification.

- Performing a leadership role that significantly shapes the future education of all healthcare practitioners as it relates to assessment based certificate programs.

Shared Governance

According to the Shared Governance Task Force which was developed in 2004, shared governance is defined as "a dynamic staff-leader partnership that promotes collaboration, shared decision-making, and accountability for improving quality of care, safety, and enhancing work life. There are many different ways to implement shared governance in nursing. Important components of a shared governance model include:

- Partnership between staff and those in leadership positions

- Inclusion of input from all relevant stakeholders

- Striving for consensus in all decisions

- Possessing a back-up plan if consensus is not possible

- Being facilitative as opposed to directive

- Attempting to listen to all perspectives

- Shared accountability

- Team ownership

- Flexibility within set boundaries

Types of Shared Governance

- Unit boards

- Clinic boards

- Committees

- Councils

- Task forces

- Nursing staff bylaws

- Input surveys

Structural Elements of Shared Governance

Studies show that the most successful shared governance bodies have a minimum of six structural elements. These include:

- A charter which outlines decision making boundaries

- Effective collaboration between staff co-chairpersons and the area manager

- Regularly scheduled meetings with a formal means of staff communication

- Mutually agreed upon agendas, which are planned by the co-chairpersons and manager and are distributed prior to meetings

- Setting of ground rules of how to work together

- Striving for consensus decisions, where everyone agrees to support decisions after various options have been discussed

- While shared governance may appear different within settings, the desired outcomes are the same. This involves a sense of being heard as well as included in decisions directly impacting nursing

Communication Strategies and Methods

Some common communication strategies and methods were already discussed in the last chapter. These strategies and methods can be extended to include effective nurse to nurse communication as well as between other members of the CV interdisciplinary team.

An effective communicator is defined as one who is capable of honestly and openly expressing their thoughts and feelings, while letting the other person openly and honestly express their thoughts and/or feelings as well. Effective communication is much more than mere politeness, mutual respect, and two individuals getting along. While these factors are important, an atmosphere which is conducive to mutual:

- Dialogue that is honest and open

- Sharing of ideas, hopes, and dreams

- Listening and hearing

- Solving of problems

Negative Impacts on Communication

On the other hand, effective communication can be hampered by an individual's bad habits. These include:

- Truth – When one person insists that they are "right" and the other person is "wrong."

- Insults – "Put-downs," such as when someone implies that the other person is a "loser" since they 'always' or 'never' do certain things.

- Passive-aggressive Behavior – When one person pouts and/or withdraws and says nothing).

- Sarcastic Behavior – When a nurse's words do not match their body language.

- "Counter-attacks" – When a nurse responds to criticism by using criticism instead of acknowledging how the other person feels)

- Diversions – When one person brings up the past instead of dealing with the present situation)

- Other blocks to effective two-way communication include:

- Giving someone unwarranted advice

- Making false assumptions

- Making value judgments

- Using clichés

- Being defensive

- Demanding an explanation

- Intentionally changing the subject

- Avoiding eye contact

- Exhibiting aggressive behavior

Essential Techniques for Good Communication

In order to create a positive atmosphere for communication among both nurses and other team members, there are five essential techniques to good communication:

1. Disarming: One person finds some truth in what the other person is saying even if they seem to be totally wrong, unreasonable, irrational and/or unfair

2. Empathy: Puts one person in the other person's shoes as well as trying to see the world through their eyes. There are two different kinds of empathy in nursing. "Thought empathy" paraphrases the other person's words while "feeling empathy" also acknowledges how they feel

3. Inquiry: One person asks gentle, probing questions in order to learn more about what the other person is thinking and/or feeling

4. Use of "I feel" statements: Express one's feelings by making use of "I feel" statements rather than "you" statements (e.g. "you're wrong" or "you make me furious")

5. Stroking: One person finds something genuinely positive to say to the other person. This indicates respect even while angry

Delegation

Delegation is defined as the assignment of authority and responsibility to another person in order to accomplish specific activities or tasks. The person who delegates the work still remains accountable for the eventual outcome of the delegated work. Two goals of delegating responsibility are to provide methods for increased work productivity as well as to empower a subordinate when making appropriate decision(s). When used appropriately, delegation is a critical nursing tool. It should always ensure safe, competent nursing care for the patient.

NCSBN Five Rights to Delegation

Within the US, the National Council of State Boards of Nursing (NCSBN) gives five rights to delegation from the perspectives of nursing service administrators and staff nurses.

- Right task

- Right circumstance

- Right person

- Right direction and communication

- Right supervision and evaluation

The Delegation Process

- Define the task

- Choose a delegate
- Determine the task
- Reach an agreement
- Monitor the delegate's progress
- Provide appropriate feedback

Strategies for Effective Delegation

- Plan ahead
- Identify necessary skills and nursing levels
- Choose the most capable person
- Clearly communicate goals
- Empower the delegate
- Set realistic deadlines and monitor the delegate progress
- Provide guidance as necessary
- Evaluate the delegates' performance
- Reward accomplishments

Results of Successful Delegation

- Making work easier
- Improving productivity and efficiency
- Increasing employee effectiveness
- Developing employees' skills and/or professional behaviors
- Ensuring that the right person does the right job

Common Errors in Delegation of Responsibility

- Over-delegating
- Under-delegating
- Inappropriate delegating

Delegation Barriers

- The "I can do it better myself" mentality
- Lack of confidence and/or trust in other workers
- Low self-confidence and/or insecurity
- Vague job descriptions
- Inadequate training
- Inadequate recruitment and/or selection
- Amount of time involved in explaining the job
- Not wanting to take the risks associated with depending on someone else
- Fear of loss of power
- Subordinate resistance to delegation
- Delegator's failure to see the subordinate's perspective
- Assigned workload is highly challenging, physically and/or mentally
- Belief that others are not capable of completing the delegated task
- Inherent resistance to authority as a result of over delegation
- Delegating to a trans-cultural work team

Delegation to Subordinates from Different Cultural Backgrounds

- Communication barriers
- Space
- Social organization
- Time
- Control of environment
- Biological variations

Communication with Interdisciplinary Team Members

Establishing and maintaining effective communication between nurses and other interdisciplinary team members, especially family doctors and specialists, can prove to be challenging.

Common Barriers to Inter-Professional Communication and Collaboration

- Personal values and expectations
- Differences in personalities
- Hierarchy
- Disruptive behavior(s)
- Culture and ethnicity
- Generational differences
- Gender differences
- Historical inter-professional and intra-professional rivalries
- Differences in language and jargon
- Differences in schedules and professional routines
- Varying degrees of preparation, qualifications, and status
- Differences in requirements, regulations, and norms of professional education
- Fear of dilution of professional identity
- Differences in accountability, payments, and rewards
- Concerns associated with clinical responsibilities
- Complexity of care
- Emphasis on rapid decision-making

Communication Guidelines for Nurses

Before contacting any other member(s) of the interdisciplinary team, the CV nurse should ask the following questions to ensure effective communication:

- Have I seen and/or assessed the patient myself before calling?
- Are there any standing orders?

- Do I have all pertinent information readily available to reference?

Chart Data for Effective Communication

- List of current meds, IV fluids and/or lab results
- Date and time tests were done as well as any previous test results for comparison
- What are the most recent vital signs?
- What is the code status?
- Have I read the most recent MD progress notes and notes from the previous shift nurse?
- Have I discussed making this phone call with my charge nurse?
- When making the call, remember to identify self, unit, patient and room number
- Know the patient's admission diagnosis and date
- Briefly state the problem, when it started and its severity
- What do I expect to happen as a result of making this phone call?
- Document the name of whom you spoke to, the time of the call, and a brief summary of the conversation
- Always engage and treat physicians and other professionals with respect

SBAR Communication Tool

Another effective communication tool is known as SBAR. It is a technique used to communicate critical information that needs immediate attention and/or action regarding a patient's condition:

- **S**ituation: What is going on with the patient? What is their current situation or problem?
- **B**ackground: What is the clinical background and/or context of the problem?
- **A**ssessment: What do I personally think the problem is? **R**ecommendation: What would I personally do to rectify the problem?

Practice Examination

Multiple-Choice Questions

1. Which of the following is NOT a component of the basic cardiac/vascular (CV) physical assessment?

A. Vital signs

B. Body weight and height

C. Skin and fingernail assessment

D. Fundoscopic assessment

Answer: D. Fundoscopic assessment

Explanation: A basic CV physical assessment will include the following observations and/or measurements: temperature, blood pressure, pulse, respirations, body weight and height, skin assessment, extremity assessment, fingernail assessment, head movement assessment, eye assessment, and cardiac and vascular assessment.

2. The CV patient's personal and family history include inquiry about all of the following issues/conditions EXCEPT:

A. Changes in color/temperature of extremities

B. Diabetes

C. History of varicosities

D. Hypertension

Answer: C. History of varicosities

Explanation: The cardiovascular patient's personal and family health history are also very important to note. Personal and/or family cardiovascular history items to take note of include the following: hypertension, myocardial infarction (MI or heart attack), high cholesterol levels, coronary artery disease (CAD), diabetes, smoking, alcohol consumption – low, moderate, heavy, amount/type of exercise, diet (in the last 24 hours to establish typical eating habits), any changes in color/temperature of extremities, any history of leg pain when walking, any history of leg sores that do not heal, and any history of blood clots.

3. Typical cardiac chest pain is often described as:

A. Feels like indigestion

B. Radiating pain to the arms, neck, back, and/or jaw

C. Sudden or gradual onset

D. All of the above

Answer: D. All of the above

Explanation: Many C/V patients will complain about chest pain at some point in time. Initially, the cause may be difficult to ascertain. Often, chest pain is precipitated and/or aggravated by things like anxiety, stress, deep breathing, exertion, and/or eating certain types of food. Chest pain can be characterized as: sudden or gradual onset, radiating to the arms, back, neck, and/or jaw, intermittent or steady, mild or severe, sharp, shooting sensation, feeling of fullness and/or heaviness, and feels like indigestion.

4. What memory mnemonic tool helps the CV nurse with the assessment of a patient's chest pain?

A. PQRST

B. ABCDE

C. LMNO

D. TUVW

Answer: A. PQRST

Explanation: Always keep possible emergency care in mind based on the severity of the patient's chest pain:

- **P** (**P**rovocative or **P**alliative) – What makes the chest pain worse or better?

- **Q** (**Q**uantity or **Q**uality) – How does the pain feel? Experiencing at the time of the examination? More/less severe than usual? How does it affect normal activities?

- **R** (**R**adiation or **R**egion) – Where in the chest is the pain located? Does it move to other areas as well?

- **S** (**S**everity) – How does the patient rate the pain on a scale of 0 to 10 with 10 being the most severe? Does it seem to reduce, intensify or same more or less the same?

- **T** (**T**iming) – When did the pain start? Did it come on suddenly or gradually? Frequency of the pain? Duration?

5. Which of the following is NOT true concerning palpitations?

A. Most palpitations are insignificant.

B. They are often the result of high blood pressure and arrhythmias.

C. They are defined as unconscious perception of the heartbeat.

D. They are usually felt over the precordium.

Answer: C. They are defined as unconscious perception of the heartbeat.

Explanation: Generally felt over the precordium (area of chest wall overlapping the great vessels and heart) and/or throat/neck area, palpitations are often defined as a conscious perception of the heartbeat. While many palpitations are insignificant, they can be the result of cardiovascular disorders such as high blood pressure, arrhythmias, mitral prolapse, and mitral stenosis.

6. Syncope typically lasts _____ and is defined as a _____ loss of consciousness.

A. Several seconds to minutes/brief

B. Several minutes to hours/complete

C. 2 to 4 hours/brief

D. 6 to 8 hours/complete

Answer: Several seconds to minutes/brief

Explanation: Usually occurring abruptly and lasting for several seconds to minutes, syncope is defined as a brief loss of consciousness, which occurs due to lack of oxygen to the brain. It can be caused from disorders such as aortic stenosis, aortic arch syndrome, and/or arrhythmias.

7. Where does intermittent claudication typically occur, and what will usually relieve it?

A. Arms/nitroglycerine

B. Legs/rest

C. Chest area/nitroglycerine

D. Neck/water

Answer: B. Legs/rest

Explanation: Intermittent claudication is defined as severe, cramping type pain of the limbs caused by exercise. This pain subsides after a few minutes of rest. Typically occurring in the legs, it can be either an acute or chronic problem.

8. Of the following questions which one is not relevant to patient inquiry regarding intermittent claudication?

A. Is the pain/cramping relieved with rest?

B. How far can you walk without any pain/cramping?

C. How do these symptoms affect your lifestyle?

D. Is this pain related to loss of bowel/bladder function?

Answer: D. Is this pain related to loss of bowel/bladder function?

Explanation: If it is an acute condition, intermittent claudication can signal acute arterial occlusion that stems from disorders such as arteriosclerosis obliterans or aortic arteriosclerotic occlusive disease. Ask the following probing questions when enquiring about a patient's intermittent claudication:

- How far can you walk without any pain and/or cramping occurring?

- How long does the pain/cramping take to subside upon resting?

- Do you need to rest more frequently than you did before?

- Is the pain-rest pattern variable?

- How does this particular symptom affect your overall lifestyle?

9. What is the cause of peripheral edema of the legs?

A. Superior vena cava syndrome

B. Excessive interstitial fluid in the tissues

C. Excessive extracellular fluid in the muscles

D. All of the above

Answer: B. Excessive interstitial fluid in the tissues

Explanation: Peripheral edema is swelling of the arms and/or legs as the result of excessive interstitial fluid within the tissues. Edema of the arms can be caused by superior vena cava syndrome or thrombophlebitis.

10. Of the following, what problem can result from impairment in cognition?

A. Personal safety risks

B. Trouble communicating with others

C. Behavioral issues

D. All of the above

Answer: D. All of the above

Explanation: Impairment in cognition can lead to many problems including: difficulties in communicating with others, personal safety risks, such as falls, limitations in self-care and activity levels as a result of fatigue, weakness, or other, inability to take part in personal care decisions, and behavioral issues. Substance use is not associated with cognitive impairment.

11. CV diseases like stroke and heart disease result in:

A. One out of every two deaths

B. One out of every three deaths

C. One out of every four deaths

D. One out of every five deaths

Answer: B. One out of every three deaths

Explanation: In the United States, approximately 1.5 million heart attacks and strokes occur every year. Cardiac/vascular diseases such as heart disease and stroke are the leading causes of death resulting in one out of every three deaths.

12. This is a tool to measure levels of intensity related to physical activity:

A. Berg Scale

B. Borg Scale

C. Pain Scale

D. Perception Scale

Answer: B. Borg Scale

Explanation: Known as the Borg Rating of Perceived Exertion (RPE) or simply the Borg Scale, this is a tool that can be used to measure levels of intensity related to physical activity. Perceived exertion is defined as how hard a person feels their body is performing at a specific time. It depends on factors such as any physical sensations experienced during periods of physical activity, such as elevated respirations, elevated heart rate, and increased level of sweating as well as muscle fatigue.

13. How much does the human adult heart weigh?

A. 8 to 10 ounces

B. 10 to 14 ounces

C. 14 to 16 ounces

D. 16 to 18 ounces

Answer: B. 10 to 14 ounces

Explanation: The human heart is about the size of an adult's fist and weighs between 10 and 14 ounces.

14. The outer heart surface, which consists of squamous epithelial cells over the top of connective tissue, is called:

A. Epicardium

B. Myocardium

C. Endocardium

D. Pericardium

Answer: A. Epicardium

Explanation: The epicardium is the outer heart surface that consists of squamous epithelial cells over the top of connective tissue. The myocardium is the middle layer which makes up the majority of the heart wall. The thickest and strongest layer, it is made up of striated muscle fibers which cause heart contractions. The endocardium is the innermost layer that lines the heart chambers. It is composed of endothelial tissue with smooth muscle bundles and small blood vessels. The pericardium is a membranous sac, referred to as the pericardium, surrounds the heart as well as the roots of the great vessels.

15. Which chamber of the heart receives deoxygenated blood from the lower part of the body via the inferior vena cava?

A. Right atrium

B. Left atrium

C. Right ventricle

D. Left ventricle

Answer: A. Right atrium

Explanation: The right atrium is the upper right chamber which receives deoxygenated blood from the lower part of the body via the inferior vena cava. The right atrium receives deoxygenated blood from the head, neck, and arms via the superior vena cava. Additionally, it serves much like a reservoir for blood, which leaves this chamber and goes into the right ventricle.

16. Which heart chamber serves as the heart's major "pumping station," as it sends blood to all body parts by way of the aorta?

A. Right atrium

B. Left atrium

C. Right ventricle

D. Left ventricle

Answer: D. Left ventricle

Explanation: The left ventricle is the lower left heart chamber which gets oxygenated blood from the left atrium. It also serves as the heart's major "pumping station," as it sends blood to all body parts by way of the aorta.

17. Found within the ventricular walls, which muscles form a tight seal in order to stop backflow when the ventricles contract?

A. Papillary muscles

B. Pericardial muscles

C. Pilar muscles

D. Septal muscles

Answer: A. Papillary muscles

Explanation: The papillary muscles are found within the ventricular walls; these muscles form a tight seal in order to stop backflow when the ventricles contract.

18. This heart valve prevents backflow of blood from the aorta into the left ventricle:

A. Mitral valve

B. Tricuspid valve

C. Aortic valve

D. Pulmonic valve

Answer: A. Mitral valve

Explanation: The mitral (bicuspid) valve stops backflow of blood from the left ventricle into the right atrium). The tricuspid valve prevents backflow from the right ventricle up into the right atrium) valves. The aortic valve prevents backflow from the aorta into the left ventricle. The pulmonic valve stops backflow of blood from the pulmonary artery into the left ventricle).

19. These vessels act as connections between two arterial branches:

A. Collateral arteries

B. Arterioles

C. Capillaries

D. Venules

Answer: A. Collateral arteries

Explanation: The collateral arteries act as connections between two arterial branches. The arterioles are tiny, thinner arterial branches that deliver blood to body tissues and control the flow of blood to the capillaries. The capillaries are tiny blood vessels with microscopic walls that join arterioles and venules.

20. How many types of arteries are there according to their function?

A. One

B. Two

C. Three

D. Four

Answer: B. Two

Explanation: Arteries can be classified by their function, with the two types being conductive arteries, such as the external iliac artery, which generally have few branches and follow fairly straight lines, and distributive arteries, which have multiple branches that spread out from the conductive arteries.

21. The largest vein in the body is the _____ and it contains _____ valves.

A. Inferior vena cava/one

B. Superior vena cava/two

C. Vena cava/zero

D. Aorta/three

Answer: C. Vena cava/zero

Explanation: The largest vein in the body is the vena cava, which returns blood to the right atrium, and contains no valves.

22. This is the largest coronary vein, and its function is to return deoxygenated blood from the myocardium to the right atrium:

A. Aorta

B. Coronary sinus

C. Coronary venule

D. Vena cava

Answer: B. Coronary sinus

Explanation: The coronary sinus is the largest coronary vein, and its function is to return deoxygenated blood from the myocardium to the right atrium. Venules have thinner walls than the arterioles and they gather blood from the capillaries.

23. Where is the SA node located?

A. Within the left atrium

B. Within the right atrium

C. Within the left ventricle

D. Within the right ventricle

Answer: Within the right atrium there are two nodes known as the sinoatrial (SA) and the atrioventricular (AV) nodes. The SA node (pacemaker) is located in the upper portion of the right atrium just below the superior vena cava opening, and it initiates and regulates the heartbeat. The SA node has a firing rate of 60 to 100 hundred beats per minute while the AV node's rate of firing is 40 to 60 beats per minute.

24. Regarding polarization, which phase involves closing of sodium channels?

A. Phase 0

B. Phase 1

C. Phase 2

D. Phase 3

Answer: B. Phase 1

Explanation:

- Phase 0: Rapid de-polarization is where sodium moves into the cell rapidly and calcium moves into the cell slowly.

- Phase 1: Early re-polarization is where the sodium channels close.

- Phase 2: Plateau is where the calcium continues to flow into the cell and potassium flows out.

- Phase 3: Rapid re-polarization is where calcium channels close and potassium flows out quickly.

- Phase 4: Resting phase involves active transportation through sodium-potassium pump starts to restore potassium to the inside and sodium to the outside of the cells, the cell membrane becomes impermeable to sodium, and the potassium may move out of the cells.

25. During this cycle, the AV valves close to prevent backflow of blood into the atria, the atria relax, the ventricles contract, and a long, low pitched S1 sound occurs:

A. Systole

B. Diastole

C. Contractility

D. Excitability

Answer: A. Systole

Explanation: The cardiac cycle is made up of two separate phases, namely systole and diastole. With systole, the AV valves close preventing backflow into the atria, the atria relax, the ventricles contract, and a long, low pitched S1 or "lub" sound occurs. With diastole, the SL valves close preventing backflow into the ventricles, the atria contract s, the ventricles relax, and a short, sharp pitched S2 or "dub" sound takes place.

26. Of the following conditions, which is NOT a contributing factor in left-sided heart failure?

A. Chronic obstructive lung disease

B. Pulmonary hypertension

C. Asthma

D. Acute respiratory distress syndrome

Answer: C. Asthma

Explanation: Left-sided heart failure is the most common type. It is often caused by valve disease, pulmonary hypertension, chronic obstructive lung disease (COPD), or acute respiratory distress syndrome (ARDS).

27. This blood test is inexpensive and assists in the diagnosis and treatment of heart failure:

A. Prothrombin time (PT) with INR

B. Complete blood cell (CBC) count

C. Brain natriuretic peptide (BNP)

D. Basic metabolic panel (BMP)

Answer: Brain natriuretic peptide (BNP)

Explanation: Brain (beta-type) natriuretic peptide (BNP) is an inexpensive blood test to assist in the determination of a treatment plan for heart failure. With this, < 100, HF is mild, 100-400, HF is moderate, and > 400, HF is definite or severe.

28. This disease results from interactions of atherosclerotic plaque, aggregation of platelets, formation of thrombi, and vasoconstriction:

A. Congestive heart failure

B. Stroke

C. Coronary artery disease

D. Myocardial infarction

Answer: C. Coronary artery disease

Explanation: Coronary artery disease (CAD) results from interactions of the following conditions: atherosclerotic plaque (narrowing and/or hardening of arteries from an excessive buildup of fatty, fibrous plaque which can eventually rupture), aggregation of platelets, formation of thrombi (clots), and vasoconstriction (narrowing of a blood vessel as a result of contraction of its muscular wall).

29. An angina "attack" typically lasts less than:

A. 3 to 5 minutes

B. 5 to 10 minutes

C. 10 to 15 minutes

D. 15 to 30 minutes

Answer: C. 10 to 15 minutes

Explanation: An episode of angina chest pain usually last around 10 to 15 minutes.

30. What are the main objectives of medical management of angina?

A. Decreasing the myocardium demand for oxygen.

B. Increasing the oxygen supply to the myocardium.

C. Preventing further cardiac damage.

D. Relieving the pain.

E. Both A and B

F. Both C and D

Answer: E. Both A and B

Explanation: The two main objectives are decreasing the myocardium's demand for oxygen and increasing oxygen supply to the myocardium.

31. Of the following, which is a red flag that the patient may have a myocardial infarction?

A. Stable angina

B. Unstable angina

C. Chest pain

D. Palpitations

Answer: B. Unstable angina

Explanation: "Stable" angina occurs on exertion and symptoms stay stable for several months. Typically, there is only slight activity limitation and stable angina is manageable with medications. "Unstable" angina is an unpredictable, transient episode of prolonged, severe discomfort which appears at rest, and symptoms mimic a myocardial infarction (MI).

32. Nitroglycerine is usually ordered:

A. Up to 2 tablets administered 10 minutes apart.

B. Up to 3 tablets administered 5 minutes apart.

C. Up to 4 tablets administered 10 minutes apart

D. Up to 5 tablets administered 5 minutes apart.

Answer: B. Up to 3 tablets administered 5 minutes apart.

Explanation: For the treatment of angina, nitroglycerine is used. The patient should always carry the tablets and place under the tongue as required. The typical dosage is up to 3 tabs administered 5 minutes apart.

33. Of the following patients, which one is likely experiencing a myocardial infarction (MI)?

A. A 72 year old woman with mild substernal pain that only lasted 3 minutes.

B. A 65 year old man with localized epigastric discomfort and cough.

C. A 68 year old man with squeezing severe substernal pain that is persistent and lasts longer than 15 minutes.

D. A 67 year old woman with chest pain relieved with one nitroglycerine.

Answer: C. A 68 year old man with squeezing severe substernal pain that is persistent and lasts longer than 15 minutes.

Explanation: Myocardial infarction pain is persistent, severe substernal pain or pain over the pericardium, which may radiate widely throughout the chest and may be accompanied by pain in the shoulders, jaw, neck, teeth, hands, and/or arms (especially left arm). It is often described as "viselike," "squeezing," and/or "crushing," and typically lasts longer than 15 minutes and can last as long as 12 hours, and occurs spontaneously or may follow an attack of unstable angina.

34. Of the following, which is NOT a risk factor for myocardial infarction?

A. Male gender

B. Age over 40 years

C. Birth control use

D. Nitroglycerine use

Answer: D. Nitroglycerine use

Explanation: The risk factors for myocardial infarction include male gender, age over 40 years, previous history of atherosclerosis, hypertension, smoking, and birth control pill use.

35. Heart attacks can be fatal in approximately _____ percent of cases in women.

A. 20

B. 30

C. 40

D. 50

Answer: C. 40

Explanation: Heart attacks are also big killers of women, with 40 percent of cases being fatal.

36. Of the following, which is considered emergency treatment for a patient who has a myocardial infarction?

A. Elevating the head of the bed or stretcher

B. Administering oxygen

C. Starting an intravenous line

D. All of the above

Explanation: For the patient who has an MI, emergency treatments initiated by a cardiac/vascular nurse include elevating head of bed/stretcher, oxygen administration, morphine sulfate to decrease patient's anxiety level and workload on the heart muscle, intravenous line for heparin and fluids, stat cardiac profile and ECG, and ASA, Plavix, and/or nitrates.

37. The prognosis of peripheral artery disease depends on:

A. The age of the patient

B. The occlusion location

C. Development of any collateral circulation

D. Amount of time between development and removal.

E. A and D

F. B, C, and D

Answer: F. B, C, and D

Explanation: The prognosis of PAD depends on the occlusion location, development of collateral circulation to make up for decreased blood flow, as well as the amount of time between development and removal of the blockage. In advanced, severe cases of peripheral artery disease, necrosis, ulceration, and/or gangrene can result.

38. Treatment for peripheral artery disease involves possible medications. Which of the following is NOT recommended for this condition?

A. Vitamin K

B. ACE inhibitors

C. Aspirin

D. Thrombolytics

Answer: A. Vitamin K

Explanation: Medications used in the treatment of peripheral artery disease include anti-platelet therapy with aspirin, ACE inhibitors, analgesics to relieve pain, and thrombolytics.

39. A 62 year old female CV patient has an ABI of 0.95. What is this result considered?

A. Below normal

B. Normal

C. Borderline PAD

D. Mild to moderate PAD

Answer: C. Borderline PAD

Explanation: Arterial brachial index score of >1.30 is below normal and often seen in patients with diabetes or renal failure or in heavy smokers. Normal ABI is 1.0 to 1.29. An ABI of 0.91 to 0.99 is borderline PAD and 0.41 to 0.90 indicates mild to moderate PAD. An ABI of .0 to 0.40 is indicative of severe PAD.

40. An ultrasound combined with endoscopy to better visualize heart structures is called:

A. Venography

B. Cardiac catheterization

C. Peripheral angiography

D. Transesophageal electrocardiography

Answer: D. Transesophageal electrocardiography

Explanation: Venography is a radiographic examination of lower extremity veins using contrast medium. Cardiac catheterization is a procedure where a catheter is passed through veins and arteries in order to perform various cardiac tests (heart/artery pressures, blood flow, valve competence, etc.). Peripheral angiography is a radiographic examination of peripheral arteries and veins using contrast medium. Transesophageal electrocardiography is an ultrasound combined with endoscopy to better visualize heart structures.

41. This type of nursing diagnosis describes vulnerable patients' responses to various normal life processes and health conditions:

A. Actual nursing diagnosis

B. Syndrome nursing diagnosis

C. Risk nursing diagnosis

D. Health-promotion nursing diagnosis

Explanation: A risk nursing diagnosis describes vulnerable patients' responses to various normal life processes and health conditions. It is supported by the presence of known risk factors. An actual nursing diagnosis is a clinical nursing judgment concerning the patient's actual experiences and responses to various normal life processes or health conditions. The health-promotion nursing diagnosis is a clinical judgment regarding a patient's, their family's health and well-being, and the community's desire or motivation to increase well-being and health potential. A syndrome nursing diagnosis is a clinical judgment that describes specific clusters of nursing diagnoses that happen together. They tend to be addressed as a group and by implementing similar interventions.

42. What is the benefit of acupuncture treatments for cardiovascular patient?

A. Reduced stress symptoms

B. Acute injuries

C. Improved circulation

D. All of the above

Answer: D. All of the above

Explanation: Acupuncture treatments can result in faster recovery times from acute injuries, reduced stress symptoms, and improved circulation in the cardiovascular patient.

43. **What component of the nursing care plan gives specific instructions for activities that will be performed on the patient?**

A. Nursing diagnoses

B. Goals

C. Nursing orders

D. Evaluation

Answer: C. Nursing orders

Explanation: Exact formatting of nursing care plans varies slightly from facility to facility. Generally, they are organized by four categories. These include nursing diagnoses, which defines appropriate patient care plan and drives interventions and patient outcomes, goals and outcomes, which are observable client responses and desired change(s) in patient's condition, nursing orders, which are specific instructions for nursing activities that will be performed to assist the patient in achieving health care goal(s), and evaluation, where the healthcare team can determine patient's progress towards achievement of goals and the nursing care plan's effectiveness.

44. **According to the Institute of Medicine (IOM), the goal component that involves listening to the patient's individual needs, values, and/or preferences in order to give high-quality care is:**

A. Patient safety

B. Effectiveness

C. Timeliness

D. Patient-centered care

Answer: D. Patient-centered care

Explanation: According to the Institute of Medicine (IOM), when formulating goals for patient outcomes and health services, six essential components should be included. These are patient safety, effectiveness, timeliness, patient-centered care, efficiency, and equity. Patient-centered care involves listening to the patient's individual needs, values and/or preferences in order to give high-quality care.

45. What is one of the main concerns regarding digoxin therapy and adverse effects of this drug?

A. Hypotension

B. Digoxin toxicity

C. Palpitations

D. Dizziness

Answer: B. Digoxin toxicity

Explanation: Digoxin (lanoxin) is a cardiac glycoside indicated for heart failure and supraventricular arrhythmias. The adverse effect of concern is digoxin toxicity, which causes nausea, vomiting, headache, irritability, abdominal pain, and impaired vision.

46. What drug used to treat heart failure is contraindicated in the acute phase of myocardial infarction (MI) and/or after an MI?

A. Milrinone

B. Digoxin

C. Procanbid

D. Quinidex

Answer: A. Milrinone

Explanation: Milrinone is a PDE inhibitor that is used to treat heart failure, and it is contraindicated in the acute phase of MI and/or after an MI. This drug is only administered IV and potassium levels must be assessed before therapy.

47. This drug is indicated for ventricular tachycardia and ventricular fibrillation, and it is administered IV only:

A. Acebutolol

B. Esmolol

C. Propranolol

D. Lidocaine

Answer: D. Lidocaine

Explanation: Lidocaine and Mexiletine are in a class of drugs used to treat ventricular arrhythmias. This class works by blocking rapid influx of sodium ions during the depolarization phase of the depolarization/re-polarization cycle, which results in reduced refractory period reducing arrhythmia risk. Acebutolol, Esmolol, and Propranolol are beta-adrenergic blockers, which slow automatic processes of the SA node, reduce conduction of AV node and pacer cells, and reduce the strength of heart contractions.

48. This drug increases the risk of digoxin toxicity and pulmonary toxicity and is indicated for life-threatening arrhythmias that are resistant to other drugs:

A. Procanbid

B. Amiodarone

C. Diltazem

D. Verapamil

Answer: B. Amiodarone

Explanation: Class 3 drugs include exact MOA not known but thought to suppress arrhythmias by converting a unidirectional block to a bidirectional block. Amiodarone is used to treat life-threatening arrhythmias that do not respond to other drugs and can increase the patient's risk for digoxin and pulmonary toxicity.

49. Which class of drugs can mask symptoms of diabetes?

A. Nitrates

B. Beta-adrenergic receptor blockers

C. Calcium channel blockers

D. Antiarrhythmic

Answer: B. Beta-adrenergic receptor blockers

Explanation: Hypoglycemia may be masked in the patient taking a beta-adrenergic receptor blocker, such as atenolol, carvedilol, and metoprolol.

50. The adverse effects of amlodipine and diltiazem include all of the following EXCEPT:

A. Orthostatic hypotension

B. Dizziness

C. Nausea and vomiting

D. Peripheral edema

Answer: C. Nausea and vomiting

Explanation: The adverse effects of amlodipine, diltiazem, and nifedipine include orthostatic hypotension, heart failure, arrhythmias, headache, dizziness, and persistent peripheral edema.

51. **Which antihypertensive class of drugs inhibits sympathetic nervous system, which causes dilation of peripheral blood vessels and lowers BP?**

A. Sympatholytic

B. Vasodilators

C. Angiotensin-converting enzyme (ACE) inhibitors

D. Angiotensin II receptor blockers (ARBs)

Answer: A. Sympatholytic

Explanation: Sympatholytic drugs inhibit the sympathetic nervous system, which causes dilation of peripheral blood vessels and lower BP. Vasodilators relax peripheral vascular smooth muscles causing dilation of vessels. Angiotensin-converting enzyme (ACE) inhibitors interrupt the renin-angiotensin-aldosterone system (RAAS). Angiotensin II receptor blockers (ARB) inhibit action of angiotensin II by attaching to tissue binding receptor sites.

52. **This drug is administered in combination with other drugs in order to treat severe hypertension, and requires that the CV nurse monitor HR and BP before and after administration?**

A. Diazoxide (Hyperstat)

B. Diltazem (Cardizem)

C. Captopril (Capoten)

D. Benazepril (Lotensin)

Answer: A. Diazoxide (Hyperstat)

Explanation: Diazoxide (Hyperstat) is administered to treat severe hypertension along with other drugs. The nurse must monitor the patient's heart rate and BP before and after giving this drug. Cardizem is a calcium channel blocker, and Capoten and Lotensin are ACE inhibitors. These drugs are no used for severe hypertension or hypertensive crisis.

53. Thiazine and diuretics like this drug can lead to all of the following adverse effects EXCEPT:

A. Hyponatremia

B. Hypokalemia

C. Hypotension

D. Hypoglycemia

Answer: D. Hypoglycemia

Explanation: Side effects of these drugs include hypokalemia, hyponatremia, hypotension, nausea, and dizziness. Also, they can lead to hyperglycemia, not hypoglycemia.

54. These drugs alter the liver's ability to synthesize vitamin K-dependent clotting factors such as prothrombin:

A. Heparins

B. Oral anticoagulants

C. Antiplatelet

D. Salicylates

Answer: B. Oral anticoagulants

Explanation: Heparins inhibit formation of fibrin and thrombin by activating anti-thrombin III, which inactivates certain factors in the intrinsic and common pathways preventing stable clot formation. Oral anticoagulants alter liver's ability to synthesize vitamin K-dependent clotting factors such as prothrombin. Antiplatelet drugs interfere with activity of platelets by decreasing sticking/clumping in the blood. Salicylates are used to prevent heart attack and stroke by thinning the blood.

55. Which anti-lipemics interfere with synthesis of cholesterol by inhibiting enzymes responsible for changing HMG-CoA to mevolonate?

A. Bile sequestering drugs

B. Fibric-acid derivatives

C. HMG-CoA reductase inhibitors (statins)

D. Cholesterol absorption inhibitors

Answer: C. HMG-CoA reductase inhibitors (statins)

Explanation: Bile sequestering drugs remove excessive bile acids from fat deposits and reduce levels of low-density lipoprotein (LDL). Fibric-acid derivatives MOA is not exactly known, but they lower triglyceride levels and increase HDL minimally. HMG-CoA reductase inhibitors (statins) interfere with synthesis of cholesterol by inhibiting enzymes responsible for changing HMG-CoA to mevolonate. Cholesterol absorption inhibitors inhibit cholesterol absorption from intestines, leading to reduction in delivery of cholesterol from the intestines to the liver, and increase clearance of cholesterol from the blood.

56. Rhabdomyolysis is affects what body structure?

A. Muscles

B. Brain

C. Skin

D. Nails

Answer: A. Muscles

Explanation: Rhabdomyolysis is a muscle wasting condition that can develop secondary to the use of fibric acid derivatives, such as atorvastatin, fluvastatin, and lovastatin.

57. All of the following medications can increase digoxin concentration in the CV patient's bloodstream EXCEPT:

A. Verapamil

B. Quinidine

C. Omeprazole

D. Diazepam

Answer: D. Diazepam

Explanation: Medications that can increase digoxin concentration in a CV patient's bloodstream include quinidine, verapamil, diltazem, amiodarone, carvediolol, omeprazole, propafenone, and spironolactone.

58. All of the following medications can decrease INR and increase a patient's risk for clotting EXCEPT:

A. Barbiturates

B. Oral contraceptives

C. Doxycycline

D. Penicillin

Answer: C. Doxycycline

Explanation: Doxycycline interferes with the patient's clotting and INR.

59. Of the following foods, which should a patient avoid while taking certain statin-based cholesterol medication, such as lovastatin and atorvastatin?

A. Grapefruit

B. Oranges

C. Wheat

D. Eggs

Answer: A. Grapefruit

Explanation: When patients eat either grapefruits or pomegranates while taking some statin-based cholesterol medications such as atorvastatin (Lipitor), lovastatin (Mevacor), and simvastatin (Zocor), it can be a dangerous mix. If cardiac/vascular patients really enjoy eating these fruits they can be treated with alternative cholesterol medications like rosuvastatin (Crestor).

60. What foods can alter the effects of warfarin (Coumadin)?

A. Green leafy vegetables

B. Oranges

C. Wheat products

D. Dairy products

Answer: A. Green leafy vegetables

Explanation: As a result of high levels of Vitamin K contained in green leafy vegetables such as spinach or kale, they can pose potential risks in cardiac/vascular patients who take warfarin (Coumadin) to prevent blood clots and/or strokes. Eating excessive amounts of these types of vegetables can counteract the effectiveness of warfarin.

61. What is one of the uses for the herbal product feverfew?

A. Possesses estrogen effects

B. Used to prevent and treat migraine headaches

C. Used to improve memory

D. Enhances the immune system

Answer: B. Used to prevent and treat migraine headaches

Explanation: Feverfew is used to prevent/treat migraine headaches, fever and/or arthritis. This drug should not be taken with Aspirin, Coumadin, NSAIDS, thrombolytics, and antiplatelet medications as doing so results in prolonged bleeding times.

62. Of the following effects, which one is NOT an effect of ginseng, a commonly used herbal product?

A. Improves mental abilities

B. Anti-inflammatory

C. Estrogen effects

D. Affects bleeding time

Answer: D. Affects bleeding time

Explanation: Ginseng is considered to be an anti-inflammatory. It possesses estrogen effects, enhances the immune system, improves physical and mental abilities, and reduces anticoagulant and NSAID therapeutic effects.

63. St. John's Wort is used to treat:

A. Mild depression

B. Major depression

C. Mild anxiety

D. Major anxiety

Answer: A. Mild depression

Explanation: St. John's Wort is used to treat mild depression. It can increase adverse CNS effects when used in combination with antidepressants and/or alcohol.

64. When doing discharge planning for the CV patient, the nurse should choose cost-effective options such as:

A. Choosing name brand drugs

B. Choosing generic drugs

C. Choosing trade name drugs

D. Choosing alternatives to drugs

Answer: B. Choosing generic drugs

Explanation: Cost-effective treatment options including choices of medications (lower priced generics) and left ventricular assist devices (LVADs) which are covered by most medical insurance plans.

65. Which is NOT a true statement regarding generic drugs?

A. Generic drugs must contain the same active ingredients as the brand name counterparts.

B. Generic drugs must contain the exactly same inactive ingredients as the brand name counterparts.

C. Generic drugs are not required to contain exactly the same inactive ingredients a the brand name counterparts.

D. All generic manufacturing, packaging, and sites for testing must pass the same specifications and standards as brand name drugs.

Answer: B. Generic drugs must contain the exactly same inactive ingredients as the brand name counterparts.

Explanation: Generic drugs must contain the same active ingredient(s), dosage form(s), strength, and administration routes as their brand name counterparts. However, generics do not necessarily have to contain exactly the same inactive ingredients. All generic manufacturing, packaging, and sites for testing have to pass the same exacting specifications and quality standards as brand name drugs. In fact, several generic drugs are manufactured in the same plants as brand name products.

66. What is the purpose of a left ventricular device?

A. Assists in the maintenance of the heart's pumping ability when it cannot function effectively on its own.

B. Assists in the maintenance of the heart's electrical signaling (SA node).

C. Assists in the maintenance of the heart's contractility and conduction.

D. Assists in blood flow through the heart's valves.

Answer: A. Assists in the maintenance of the heart's pumping ability when it cannot function effectively on its own.

Explanation: A left ventricular assist device, also known as an LVAD, is a mechanical "pump-type" unit that is operated by an external battery and control system. It is surgically implanted into the cardiac/vascular patient's chest cavity assisting in the maintenance of the heart's pumping ability when it cannot function effectively on its own.

67. According to the American Heart Association, LVADs can reduce the risk of death in patients with end-stage HF by:

A. 20 percent

B. 30 percent

C. 40 percent

D. 50 percent

Answer: D. 50 percent.

Explanation: LVADs reduce the risk of death in patients with end-stage HF by at least 50 percent, at six and twelve months, and extend their average life span from approximately three months to over ten months.

68. Instructions given to a patient's doctor and loved ones concerning the type of care desired if the patient becomes unable to speak for him or herself are:

A. Patient indirectives

B. Advanced directives

C. End of life care

D. Palliative care

Answer: B. Advanced directives

Explanation: Advanced healthcare directives are instructions given to a patient's doctor and loved ones concerning the type of care desired if the patient becomes unable to speak for him or herself. These types of directives include "do not resuscitate," "do not intubate," and "no ventilator support."

69. Durable power of attorney:

A. Is a legal document that expresses specific medical care wishes.

B. Allows a patient to choose a health care agent.

C. Specifies organ donation.

D. Gives doctors the ability to decide end of life care.

Answer: B. Allows a patient to choose a health care agent.

Explanation: The durable power of attorney allows a person to choose a health care agent. Whomever is delegated the patient's health care agent has the legal right to make medical treatment decisions on behalf of the patient at the end of life or anytime the patient is incapable of speaking on their own behalf.

70. Which procedure involves permanent insertion of a small wire mesh tube into an artery to reduce the chances of further narrowing?

A. Cardiac angioplasty

B. Coronary artery stenting

C. Coronary bypass grafting

D. Coronary scaffing

Answer: B. Coronary artery stenting

Explanation: Coronary bypass grafting is a type of heart surgery, and percutaneous coronary intervention procedures (PCI) include angioplasty (a procedure used to open a clogged artery), and stenting, which involves permanent insertion of a small wire mesh tube into an artery to reduce the chances of further narrowing.

71. What phase of cardiac rehabilitation includes gradually increased levels of exercises plus other services that often include stress management, nutritional and/or smoking cessation counseling?

A. Phase I

B. Phase II

C. Phase III

D. Phase IV

Answer: B. Phase II

Explanation: Phase I begins in hospital with the gradual resumption of activities of daily living as well as walking, stair climbing and range of motion exercises. Phase II starts after discharge from the hospital and is normally done within an outpatient setting. Phase II includes gradually increased levels of exercises plus other services that often include stress management, nutritional and/or smoking cessation counseling. Phase III/Phase IV stresses a long-term maintenance and conditioning program to follow for the rest of the patient's life.

72. How often should the CV nurse teach a patient to check his or her weight?

A. Once each week

B. Two times each week

C. Three times each week

D. Daily

Answer: C. Three times each week

Explanation: The CV nurse should instruct the patient with heart failure to obtain personal weight three times (or more) per week, and to keep a record and report 3 to 5 pound gains in one week to their doctor.

73. Discharge instructions for the patient with acute coronary syndrome include all of the following EXCEPT:

A. Control stress levels

B. Avoid the cold

C. Alternate periods of activity with rest

D. Eat a diet high in fat

Answer: D. Eat a diet high in fat

Explanation: Prior to discharge from hospital, the CV nurse should advise and teach the ACS patient regarding his or her condition. These include suggestions to: alternate periods of activity and rest, avoid the cold, control stress levels, participate in a stepped cardiac rehabilitation program, progressively resume sexual activity, but may need to take nitroglycerine beforehand to avoid angina symptoms, report any chest pain (typical or atypical) to the CV nurse or physician, stop smoking immediately and never start again, and refer to a local smoking cessation program, and discuss an appropriate diet with a hospital dietician including foods to avoid.

74. What does the AHA Stroke Outcome Classification (AHA.SOC) score do?

A. It classifies the extent and severity of cardiac impairments

B. It classifies the extent and severity of vascular impairments

C. It classifies the extent and severity of neurological impairments

D. It classifies the extent and severity of pulmonary impairments

Answer: C. It classifies the extent and severity of neurological impairments

Explanation: The AHA Stroke Outcome Classification (AHA.SOC) score classifies the extent and severity of neurological impairments, which are considered to be the basis for disability.

75. Which level of the AHA Stroke Outcome Classification (AHA.SOC) is mild to moderate deficit that results from stroke in >1 domain(s)?

A. Level A

B. Level B

C. Level C

D. Level D

Answer: B. Level B

Explanation: Level A: No to minimal neurological deficit due to stroke within any domain. Level B: Mild to moderate deficit resulting from stroke in ≥ 1 domain(s). Level C: Severe deficit resulting from stroke in ≥ 1 domain(s).

76. Which level of activity involves basic activities of daily living but partially dependent in routine instrumental activities of daily living?

A. Level I

B. Level II

C. Level III

D. Level IV

Answer: B. Level II

Explanation:

- Level I: Independent - involves Basic Activities of Daily Living (i.e. BADL) and Instrumental Activities of Daily Living (i.e. IADL) tasks and/or activities patient had prior to stroke.

- Level II: Independent - involves BADL but partially dependent in routine IADL. Stroke patient is capable of living alone but needs help or supervision to access their local community.

- Level III: Partially Dependent - involves BADL (< 3 areas) and IADL. This person is capable of living independently with substantial daily help from family and/or community resources for more difficult BADL (e.g. dressing, bathing, climbing stairs, etc.).

- Level IV: Partially Dependent - involves BADL (≥ 3 areas). Stroke patient is not capable of living alone safely.

- Level V: Completely Dependent - involves BADL (≥ 5 areas) and IADL. Individual is incapable of living on their own safely. Needs care on a full-time basis.

77. Successful management of cardiac/vascular conditions requires compliance on the part of:

A. The patient

B. Family

C. The caregivers

D. All of the above

Answer: D. All of the above

Explanation: All people in the patient's life must be involved in the care.

78. Research studies have shown that using various interventions actually reduce cardiovascular events and related deaths by at least:

A. 20 percent

B. 30 percent

C. 40 percent

D. 50 percent

Answer: D. 50 percent

Explanation: Research studies have shown that using various interventions actually reduce cardiovascular events and related deaths by at least 50 percent.

79. Crisis counseling interventions may include all the following EXCEPT:

A. Taking the extra time to quietly talk to patients and their families about their current and ongoing worries and issues.

B. Showing them how to do relaxation and visualization exercises.

C. Playing quiet, relaxing music.

D. Discussing the traumatic event in detail with the patient.

Answer: D. Discussing the traumatic event in detail with the patient.

Explanation: The CV nurse should not discuss the details of the traumatic event with the patient.

80. This is one of the first coping mechanisms that patients use during highly stressful events like acute chest pain episodes:

A. Denial

B. Acceptance

C. Communication

D. Stress

Answer: A. Denial

Explanation: Studies have shown that using denial has long-term detrimental effects on cardiovascular disease outcomes and at certain critical points in time, such as during an acute cardiovascular event. One of the greatest dangers is that denial can contribute to negative cardiovascular outcomes. Patients may deny that a cardiac event is occurring. Denial is actually one of the first coping mechanisms that patients use during highly stressful events like acute chest pain episodes.

81. Which type of verbal communication focuses on seeking a specific answer?

A. Open-ended questioning

B. Closed questioning

C. Re-stating

D. Stating

Answer: B. Closed questioning

Explanation: Closed questioning focuses on seeking a specific answer. Open-ended questioning does not need a specific answer which allows patients to elaborate freely. Re-stating is repeating to the patient what is understood to be their main point.

82. Which type of non-verbal communications involves listening and giving the speaker full attention?

A. Passive

B. Active

C. Aggressive

D. Sedative

Answer: B. Active

Explanation: Non-verbal communication involves communicating without the use of words and body language. It still conveys listening, interest, and caring. This includes active (listening and giving full attention to speaker), and passive (no feedback but communication is accomplished via eye contact and/or nodding).

83. When caring for patients with Mexican heritage, the CV nurse should understand that which of the following may be true?

A. The patient will refuse to speak to people of the opposite sex.

B. The patient will only speak Spanish.

C. The family will not want to be involved with the care.

D. The patient and family may believe in biomedical and folk healers, as well as rituals and health care models.

Answer: D. The patient and family may believe in biomedical and folk healers, as well as rituals and health care models.

Explanation: The Mexican/Spanish patient and family may speak both Spanish and English. Also, the family expects to help with care, and members may take turns around the clock.

84. **Every year, deaths occur in hospital settings as a result of the spread of infections, so all health care workers must eliminate risks by practicing effective:**

A. Safety measures

B. Infection control

C. Hand washing

D. Risk management

Answer: B. Infection control

Explanation: The single most effective method of stopping the spread of germs and associated infections is the use of frequent, proper hand washing techniques. Other steps health care workers can take include coughing and/or sneezing into the sleeves, NOT the hands, keeping all immunizations up-to-date, using gloves, masks and protective clothing, making tissues and hand cleaners available for all staff and visitors to use, and following institutional guidelines concerning the handling of blood products and/or contaminated items.

85. **Infection associated with endocarditis is:**

A. Bacterial

B. Fungal

C. Both A and B

D. Neither A nor B

Answer: C. Both A and B

Explanation: Endocarditis is an infection of the heart's endocardium, valves and/or cardiac prosthesis resulting from an invasion of either bacteria or fungus. Fibrin and platelets cluster on valve tissues engulfing the circulating bacteria or fungus. This process produces vegetation which can cover the surfaces of the valves leading to deformities and/or destruction of the valve tissues.

86. Of the following conditions, which one does NOT predispose a patient to endocarditis?

A. Congenital heart disease

B. Cardiac malformation

C. Damaged heart valves

D. Myocardial infarction

Answer: D. Myocardial infarction

Explanation: Patients with certain cardiac conditions, such as valvular disease, congenital heart disease, and cardiac malformations, are predisposed to endocarditis. Thus, these persons are at an increased risk for bacterial endocarditis when they undergo open heart surgeries.

87. Cardiac/vascular patients who have prosthetic heart valve placement procedures are at an increased risk for bacterial endocarditis. Therefore, what should be given?

A. Prophylactic antibiotics before surgery.

B. Prophylactic antibiotics during surgery.

C. Prophylactic antibiotics after surgery.

D. All of the above

Answer: B. Prophylactic antibiotics during surgery.

Explanation: Antibiotics are given during surgery as a prophylactic measure.

88. Accessible, multidimensional quality measures that can be used to gauge health care performance are:

A. Quality measures

B. Quality evidence

C. Quality indicators

D. Quality variations

Answer: C. Quality indicators

Explanation: Quality indicators (QIs) were developed by the Agency for Healthcare Research and Quality (AHRQ), and they are a response to the need for accessible, multidimensional quality measures that can be used to gauge health care performance. QIs are evidence based and can be utilized to identify variations in the quality of care given on an inpatient and outpatient basis.

89. These quality indicators identify ambulatory care sensitive conditions:

A. Prevention quality indicators

B. Inpatient quality indicators

C. Patient safety indicators

D. Pediatric quality indicators

Answer: A. Prevention quality indicators

Explanation: Prevention quality indicators (PQIs) identify ambulatory care sensitive conditions (i.e. conditions where good outpatient care can possibly prevent the need for hospitalization and/or early intervention may prevent complications or the development of more severe disease).

90. Pediatric quality indicators (PDIs) reflect quality of care for children under:

A. 15 years of age

B. 16 years of age

C. 17 years of age

D. 18 years of age

Answer: C. 17 years of age

Explanation: Pediatric quality indicators (PDIs) reflect quality of care for children under 17 years of age and newborns inside hospitals. These QIs identify possible avoidable hospitalizations among children (i.e. area-level indicators).

91. Which certifying body is an affiliate of the American Nurses Association (ANA), and conducts certification examinations?

A. The American Center for Credentialing

B. The State Board of Nursing

C. The American Nurses Credentialing Center

D. The Nurse Practice Center

Answer: C. The American Nurses Credentialing Center

Explanation: The American Nurses Credentialing Center (ANCC) is an affiliate of the ANA that conducts certification examinations as well as certifies advanced practice nurses. The State Board of Nursing is the appointed body responsible for the administration of the Nursing Practice Act within each state.

92. An experienced, trusted adviser who acts as a coach, advisor, and counselor to another colleague is called a:

A. Protégé

B. Mentor

C. Supporter

D. Adviser

Answer: B. Mentor

Explanation: A mentor is defined as an experienced, trusted adviser who acts as a coach, advisor, friend, cheerleader, and counselor to another colleague.

93. Of the five essential techniques for communication, when one person puts him or herself in the other person's shoes as well as trying to see the world through their eyes, this is called:

A. Disarming

B. Empathy

C. Inquiry

D. Stroking

Answer: B. Empathy

Explanation: Disarming is where one person finds some truth in what the other person is saying even if they seem to be totally wrong, unreasonable, irrational and/or unfair. Empathy is where one person puts one person in the other person's shoes as well as trying to see the world through their eyes. There are two different kinds of empathy in nursing. "Thought empathy" paraphrases the other person's words while "feeling empathy" also acknowledges how they feel. Inquiry is where one person asks gentle, probing questions in order to learn more about what the other person is thinking and/or feeling. Stroking is where one person finds something genuinely positive to say to the other person.

94. Regarding communication and the SBAR technique/tool, the B stands for:

A. Barrier

B. Bedside

C. Background

D. Breakthrough

Answer: C. Background

Explanation: The SBAR is a technique used to communicate critical information that needs immediate attention and/or action regarding a patient's condition. S is for situation, B is for background, A is for assessment, and R is for reassessment.

95. A 68 year old Caucasian female patient has a pulse oximetry reading of 76%. She is talkative, has normal skin color, and does not appear to be in distress. What could cause this false low reading?

A. A recent blood transfusion

B. A temperature of 99.9 F

C. Nail polish on the finger

D. Recent exposure to chemicals

Answer: C. Nail polish on the finger

Explanation: Nail polish of the finger can give a low pulse oximetry reading. Reduced body temperature and circulatory impairment can also cause low readings.

96. **The CV nurse is caring for a patient with tachycardia, tachypnea, pulmonary edema, fever, and cough with frothy sputum. Based on these findings, what can you expect to be ordered?**

A. Oxygen, calcium channel blockers, and morphine

B. Nitroglycerine, morphine, and loop diuretics

C. Thiazide diuretics and oxygen

D. Thiazide diuretics, angiotensin-converting enzyme inhibitors, and oxygen

Answer: B. Nitroglycerine, morphine, and loop diuretics

Explanation: Common initial treatment for acute pulmonary edema involves nitroglycerine to reduce preload, morphine to reduce anxiety, and loop diuretics (such as furosemide) to promote diuresis.

97. **For stage I hypertension, first-line drugs include:**

A. Thiazide diuretics

B. Loop diuretics

C. Calcium channel blockers

D. Angiotensin-converting enzyme inhibitors

Answer: A. Thiazide diuretics

Explanation: Thiazide diuretics are first-line treatment for stage I hypertension. A two-drug combination is used to treat stage II hypertension, consisting of a thiazide diuretic and an ACE inhibitor, beta blocker, ARB, or calcium channel blocker.

98. Premature ventricular contractions (PVCs) can be caused from all of the following EXCEPT:

A. Mitral valve prolapse

B. Metabolic alkalosis

C. Hypoxia

D. Infection

Answer: B. Metabolic alkalosis

Explanation: PVCs are caused by anesthetics, electrolyte imbalances, hypoxia, ventricular hypertrophy, increased sympathetic stimulation, metabolic acidosis (not alkalosis), myocarditis, mitral valve prolapse, myocardial ischemia/infarction, tobacco use, caffeine, alcohol, and various sympathomimetic drugs (epinephrine and isoproterenol).

99. A slow ventricular rate can decrease cardiac output and cause:

A. Chest pain and palpitations

B. Facial numbness and hypertension

C. Dizziness and hypotension

D. Cyanosis and claudication

Answer: C. Dizziness and hypotension

Explanation: Atrioventricular blocks slow the ventricular rate and lead to confusion, hypotension, and dizziness.

100. What block occurs when some of the electrical impulses from the AV node are blocked and some are conducted through normal conduction pathways?

A. Atrioventricular block

B. First-degree atrioventricular block

C. Second-degree atrioventricular block

D. Third-degree atrioventricular block

Answer: C. Second-degree atrioventricular block

Explanation: Second-degree AV blocks can be of Type I or Type II, and they typically resolve when the underlying condition.

101. Aortic stenosis can occur from all of the following EXCEPT:

A. Congenital stenosis of the pulmonic valve

B. Rheumatic fever

C. Atherosclerosis

D. Left-sided heart failure

Answer: D. Left-sided heart failure

Explanation: Usually after age 70 years, left-sided heart failure occurs as a complication of aortic stenosis, but it is not a cause of it. Other causes include coarctation of the aorta.

102. What is a known complication of pulmonic stenosis?

A. Right-sided heart failure

B. Left-sided heart failure

C. Myocardial ischemia

D. Pulmonic insufficiency

Answer: A. Right-sided heart failure

Explanation: Pulmonic stenosis is the result of hardening or narrowing of the opening between the right ventricle and the pulmonary artery. A known complication is right-sided heart failure.

103. Mitral insufficiency is the result of:

A. Damaged mitral valve allows blood from the right ventricle to flow back into the right atrium during systole.

B. Damaged mitral valve allows blood from the left ventricle to flow back into the left atrium during systole.

C. Damaged mitral valve allows blood from the right atrium to flow back into the right ventricle during diastole.

D. Damaged mitral valve allows blood from the left atrium to flow back into the left ventricle during diastole.

Answer: B. Damaged mitral valve allows blood from the left ventricle to flow back into the left atrium during systole.

Explanation: Mitral insufficiency occurs when a damaged mitral valve allows blood from the left ventricle to flow back into the left atrium during systole. As a result, the atrium enlarges to accommodate the backflow and the left ventricle dilates to accommodate the increased blood volume.

104. A junctional beat that comes from the AV junction before the next expected sinus beat is called:

A. A premature junctional contraction

B. A premature ventricular contraction

C. An AV junctional contraction

D. An AV premature contraction

Answer: A. A premature junctional contraction

Explanation: A premature junctional contraction (PVC) is a junctional beat from the AV junction, and it interrupts the underlying rhythm.

105. Which of the following patients is at risk for developing severe heart failure?

A. A 70 year old white male in atrial fibrillation with hypertrophic cardiomyopathy

B. A 78 year old black female in atrial fibrillation with rheumatic heart disease

C. A 72 year old white female in atrial fibrillation with mitral stenosis

D. All of the above

Answer: D. All of the above

Explanation: patients with preexisting cardiac disease tend to tolerate atrial fibrillation poorly and usually develop severe heart failure. These conditions include hypertrophic cardiomyopathy, rheumatic heart disease, mitral stenosis, and prosthetic mitral valves.

106. In patients with hypertrophic cardiomyopathy, cardiac output may be:

A. Low

B. Normal

C. High

D. All of the above

Answer: D. All of the above

Explanation: In patients with hypertrophic cardiomyopathy, cardiac output can be low, normal, or high, and this depends on whether the stenosis is obstructive.

107. This arrhythmia usually presents as bradycardia, with episodes of sinus arrest and SA block along with sudden and brief episodes of rapid atrial fibrillation:

A. Sinoatrial exit block

B. Sick sinus syndrome

C. Sinus arrhythmia

D. Sinus arrest

Answer: B. Sick sinus syndrome

Explanation: Sick sinus syndrome (SSS) occurs in patients who are prone to paroxysm of other atrial tachyarrhythmias, such as atrial flutter and ectopic atrial tachycardia.

108. In which type of atrial tachycardia does the arrhythmia occur as a transient event in which the rapid heart rate appears and disappears suddenly?

A. Paroxysmal atrial tachycardia (PAT)

B. Multifocal atrial tachycardia (MAT)

C. Atrial tachycardia with block

D. AV tachycardia

Answer: A. Paroxysmal atrial tachycardia (PAT)

Explanation: PAT is a type of tachycardia that appears and disappears suddenly. MAT, or chaotic atrial rhythm, originates from multiple foci.

109. Of the following, which is NOT a typical cause of a wandering pacemaker?

A. Increased parasympathetic influences on the SA node

B. Loop diuretics

C. Valvular heart disease

D. Digoxin toxicity

Answer: B. Loop diuretics

Explanation: A wandering pacemaker is caused by increased parasympathetic influences on the SA node and/or the AV junction. It is also caused by atrial tissue inflammation, digoxin toxicity, chronic pulmonary disease, and valvular heart disease.

110. Sinus bradycardia is caused by all of the following drugs EXCEPT:

A. Beta blockers

B. Lithium

C. Quinidine

D. Benazepril

Answer: D. Benazepril

Explanation: Several drugs can cause a slow heartbeat, such as beta blockers, calcium channel blockers, lithium, sotalol, amiodarone, propafenone, and quinidine.

111. Medical and clinical conditions that can cause sinus tachycardia include all of the following EXCEPT:

A. Shock

B. Asthma

C. Sepsis

D. Hyperthyroidism

Answer: B. Asthma

Explanation: Sinus tachycardia is caused by heart failure, cardiogenic shock, pericarditis, shock, anemia, respiratory distress, pulmonary embolism, sepsis, and hyperthyroidism.

112. This arrhythmia occurs when all of the heart's higher pacemakers fail or when supraventricular impulses cannot reach the ventricles because of some type of block:

A. Idioventricular rhythm

B. Accelerated junctional rhythm

C. Junctional escape rhythm

D. Wandering pacemaker

Answer: A. Idioventricular rhythm

Explanation: Idioventricular rhythm is also called ventricular escape rhythm, and it acts as a safety mechanism to prevent asystole (ventricular standstill).

113. Third-degree AV block occurring at the infra-nodal level is usually associated with:

A. Extensive anterior MI

B. Extensive inferior MI

C. Mitral valve stenosis

D. Pulmonary valve stenosis

Answer: A. Extensive anterior MI

Explanation: Third-degree AV block occurs at the anatomic level of the AV node and can result from increased parasympathetic tone, which is associated with inferior wall MI. AT the infra-nodal level, AV block is associated with anterior MI.

114. What is one method of treatment for a patient who has an arrhythmia that does not respond to drug therapy?

A. Synchronized cardioversion

B. Vascular brachytherapy

C. Stenting

D. Grafting

Answer: A. Synchronized cardioversion

Explanation: Cardioversion is an elective procedures used to correct tachyarrhythmias, such as atrial flutter, atrial tachycardia, atrial fibrillation, and symptomatic ventricular tachycardia.

115. Of the following, which patient would NOT be a candidate for a permanent pacemaker?

A. A 66 year old man with Wolff-Parkinson-White syndrome

B. A 32 year old female with sick sinus syndrome

C. A 45 year old man with complete heart block

D. A 58 year old woman with atrial fibrillation

Answer: D. A 58 year old woman with atrial fibrillation

Explanation: Patients with persistent bradycardia, complete heart block, congenital heart disease, Stokes-Adams syndrome, Wolff-Parkinson-White syndrome, and sick sinus syndrome are candidates for a permanent pacemaker.

116. Left atrial ablation and ablation for persistent atrial flutter are contraindicated if:

A. The patient has had a recent MI.

B. The patient has atherosclerosis.

C. The patient has a diseased heart valve.

D. The patient has an atrial thrombus.

Answer: D. The patient has an atrial thrombus.

Explanation: Left atrial ablation and ablation for persistent atrial flutter are contraindicated if the patient has an atrial thrombus. Left ventricular ablation is contraindicated if the patient has a left ventricular thrombus. Ablation catheters are not inserted through a mechanical prosthetic heart.

117. How do alpha-adrenergic receptor blockers work?

A. They occupy special receptor sites on the smooth muscle of blood vessels.

B. They prevent stimulation of the sympathetic nervous system.

C. They stimulate local or systemic constriction of blood vessels.

D. They stimulate the nervous system, increase heart rate, and constrict blood vessels.

Answer: A. They occupy special receptor sites on the smooth muscle of blood vessels.

Explanation: Alpha-adrenergic receptor blockers relax the smooth muscle of the blood vessels to dilate them and decrease blood pressure. Beta-adrenergic receptor blockers prevent stimulation of the sympathetic nervous system. Non-catecholamines stimulate local or systemic constriction of blood vessels. Catecholamines stimulate the nervous system, constrict peripheral blood vessels, increase heart rate, and dilate the bronchi.

118. Tricuspid insufficiency occurs when:

A. The tricuspid valve is open all the time.

B. The tricuspid valve is closed all the time.

C. The tricuspid valve doesn't close completely and this allows blood to flow back into the left atrium.

D. The tricuspid valve doesn't close completely and this allows blood to flow back into the right atrium.

Answer: D. The tricuspid valve doesn't close completely and this allows blood to flow back into the right atrium.

Explanation: With tricuspid insufficiency, the tricuspid valve does not completely shut, and therefore, blood flows into the right atrium from the right ventricle.

119. All of the following are complication of dilated cardiomyopathy EXCEPT:

A. Intermittent claudication

B. Intractable heart failure

C. Arrhythmias

D. Emboli

Answer: A. Intermittent claudication

Explanation: Syncope and sudden death occur from ventricular arrhythmias that are seen with dilated cardiomyopathy.

120. Regarding the Jones criteria for diagnosing rheumatic fever, which of the following is considered "major" criteria?

A. Fever

B. Subcutaneous nodules

C. Arthralgia

D. Prolonged PR interval

Answer: B. Subcutaneous nodules

Explanation: Major criteria include carditis, migratory polyarthritis, Sydenham's chorea, subcutaneous nodules, and erythema marginatum. Minor criteria include fever, arthralgia, elevated acute phase reactants, and prolonged PR interval.

121. Common causes of aortic insufficiency include all of the following EXCEPT:

A. Endocarditis

B. Hypertension

C. Syphilis

D. Gonorrhea

Answer: D. Gonorrhea

Explanation: Aortic insufficiency is caused by rheumatic fever, syphilis, hypertension, endocarditis, or trauma.

122. What would the CV nurse expect to find on a chest x-ray of a patient with aortic insufficiency?

A. Ventricular enlargement

B. Pulmonary vein congestion

C. Cardiomyopathy

D. A and B

Answer: D. A and B

Explanation: Chest x-ray of the patient with aortic insufficiency will show ventricular enlargement and pulmonary vein congestion.

123. The CV nurse should expect to see all of the following on an ECG of a patient with severe aortic insufficiency EXCEPT:

A. ST segment depressions

B. Sinus tachycardia

C. T-wave inversions

D. Prolonged PR interval

Answer: D. Prolonged PR interval

Explanation: ECG will show sinus tachycardia, left ventricular hypertrophy, left atrial hypertrophy, ST segment depressions, and T wave inversions in the patient with severe aortic insufficiency.

124. Crisis counseling for the patient with psychological concerns who has suffered an emergency cardiac/vascular event can:

A. Reduce the chances of the patient dying.

B. Reduce the chances of a repeat cardiovascular event.

C. Reduce associated hospital visits.

D. All of the above

Answer: D. All of the above

Explanation: Rather than just using biomedical therapies during an emergency cardiac/vascular event, there is also a great deal of benefit in providing crisis counseling including certain psychological interventions. Doing so can ease immediate anxiety and stress in patients and their family/caregivers at the time of an event. However, it can also reduce the chances of patients dying or having repeat cardiovascular events with fewer associated hospital visits.

125. A psychological coping strategy, or basic defense mechanism, that enables individuals to engage in certain risky types of behavior with little or no conscious awareness of the consequences is:

A. Denial

B. Acceptance

C. Bargaining

D. Criticism

Answer: A. Denial

Explanation: Denial can be defined as a psychological coping strategy, or basic defense mechanism, that enables individuals to engage in certain risky types of behavior with little or no conscious awareness of the consequences. For example, patients can deny the existence of a newly diagnosed heart disease.

126. The nurse asks the patient, "How does that make you feel?" What type of communication is this?

A. Closed questioning

B. Open-ended questioning

C. Stating

D. Re-stating

Answer: B. Open-ended questioning

Explanation: Closed questioning focuses on seeking a specific answer. Open-ended questioning does not need a specific answer which allows patients to elaborate freely. Re-stating involves repeating to the patient what is understood to be their main point. Stating is simply saying something to the patient.

127. The nurse smiles and nods to the CV patient. What type of non-verbal communication is this?

A. Active

B. Passive

C. Distant

D. Close

Answer: B. Passive

Explanation: Non-verbal communication involves communicating without the use of words and body language. It still conveys listening, interest, and caring. This includes active (listening and giving full attention to speaker) and passive (no feedback but communication is accomplished via eye contact and/or nodding).

128. To handle a language barrier, the CV nurse can:

A. Keep communication simple

B. Act things out

C. Get a translator

D. All of the above

Explanation: All of these actions are measures to deal with language barriers.

129. Which of the following is NOT one of the stages of grief and loss?

A. Anger

B. Bargaining

C. Denial

D. Inversion

Answer: D. Inversion

Explanation: The five stages of grief and loss include denial, anger, bargaining, depression, and acceptance.

130. According to the AHA, a reasonable approach to endocarditis prophylaxis should take all the following factors into consideration EXCEPT:

A. Degree that the patient's underlying condition creates endocarditis risk.

B. Apparent risk of bacteremia during the procedure.

C. Possible adverse effects of the prophylactic agent being used.

D. All of the above

Answer: D. All of the above

Explanation: Additional approaches include overall cost-benefit aspects of the recommended prophylactic antibiotic regimen.

131. The quality indicators that focus on potentially preventable complication instances and other medical treatment events resulting from health care system exposure are:

A. Prevention quality indicators

B. Inpatient quality indicators

C. Patient safety indicators

D. Pediatric quality indicators

Answer: C. Patient safety indicators

Explanation: Quality indicators (QIs) were developed by the Agency for Healthcare Research and Quality (AHRQ), and they are a response to the need for accessible, Patient safety indicators (PSIs) focus on potentially preventable complication instances and other medical treatment events resulting from health care system exposure.

132. The CV patient has the right to all of the following EXCEPT:

A. Be informed about care alternatives.

B. Confidential communication.

C. Receive information about his or her healthcare.

D. Receive information about the finances of the healthcare facility.

Answer: D. Receive information about the finances of the healthcare facility.

Explanation: All patients have the right to:

- Considerate, respectful care,
- Receive enough information to make informed consent
- Receive information about care alternatives
- Refuse (treatments),
- Privacy,
- Confidential communication
- Expect a hospital to make a reasonable response to their request for service
- Receive information about human experimentation
- Expect reasonable continuity of care
- Receive/examine an explanation of a hospital invoice
- Know a hospital's rules/regulations

133. What document explicates the goals, values, and ethical precepts that direct the profession of nursing?

A. ANA Code for Nurses

B. ANA Standards of Care for Nurses

C. ANCC Code for Nurses

D. ANCC Standards of Care for Nurses

Answer: A. ANA Code for Nurses

Explanation: The American Nurses Association (ANA) *Code for Nurses with Interpretive Statements* (Code for Nurses) explicates the goals, values, and ethical precepts that direct the profession of nursing. The ANA believes the *Code for Nurses* is nonnegotiable and that each nurse has an obligation to uphold and adhere to the code of ethics.

134. The appointed body responsible for the administration of the Nursing Practice Act within each state is:

A. The American Nurses Association (ANA)

B. The American Nurses Credentialing Center (ANCC)

C. The State Board of Nursing

D. The Nurses Administration Board

Answer: C. The State Board of Nursing

Explanation: The State Board of Nursing is the appointed body responsible for the administration of the Nursing Practice Act within each state.

135. The nursing professionals who are paired with newly hired nurses and play active roles in the orientation process to the new clinical setting are called:

A. Mentors

B. Preceptors

C. Counselors

D. Educators

Answer: B. Preceptors

Explanation: Unlike mentors, trained preceptors are paired with newly hired nurses and play active roles in the orientation process to the new clinical setting. Preceptors act as educators, role models, socializers, friends, and confidantes.

136. A dynamic staff-leader partnership that promotes collaboration, shared decision-making, and accountability for improving quality of care, safety, and enhancing work life is:

A. Shared governance

B. Shared relevance

C. Shared enhancement

D. Shared decisions

Answer: A. Shared governance

Explanation: According to the Shared Governance Task Force which was developed in 2004, shared governance is defined as "a dynamic staff-leader partnership that promotes collaboration, shared decision-making, and accountability for improving quality of care, safety, and enhancing work life."

137. Regarding components of communication, when one person finds some truth in what the other person is saying even if they seem to be totally wrong, unreasonable, irrational, and/or unfair, it is called:

A. Disarming

B. Empathy

C. Inquiry

D. Stroking

Answer: A. Disarming

Explanation: When one person finds some truth in what the other person is saying even if they seem to be totally wrong, unreasonable, irrational, and/or unfair, it is called disarming. Empathy puts one person in the other person's shoes as well as trying to see the world through their eyes. Inquiry is where one person asks gentle, probing questions in order to learn more about what the other person is thinking and/or feeling. Stroking is where one person finds something genuinely positive to say to the other person. This indicates respect even while angry.

138. In this stage of group dynamics, group members and the facilitator/teacher start to share ideas, thoughts and beliefs with each other:

A. Forming

B. Norming

C. Storming

D. Performing

Answer: B. Norming

Explanation: The characteristics of group learning include "forming", "norming", "storming", "performing", "adjourning" and "mourning." In the norming stage, group members and the facilitator/teacher start to share ideas, thoughts and beliefs with each other. They also develop shared norms as well as establish rules for group interactions. It is the responsibility of the teacher to help clarify ideas and/or ground rules, encourage quieter and/or shy patients to participate and move the group along towards its defined purpose.

139. The MICRO-Q consists of:

A. Questions about the patient's health status.

B. Statements regarding the patient's knowledge of risk factors, diet, lifestyle, and pre-admission delays.

C. Statements about the patient's family history.

D. Questions about the patient's lab work, diagnostic tests, and lifestyle choices.

Answer: B. Statements regarding the patient's knowledge of risk factors, diet, lifestyle, and pre-admission delays.

Explanation: It is a simple, efficient, reliable outcome measurement indicator. The MICRO-Q consists of 26 statements where 18 of the statements are true and the other 8 statements are false. These statements include knowledge of risk factors, diet, lifestyle, pre-admission avoidable delays as well as cardiac disease knowledge. A patient responds to these statements with "true", "false", or "don't know."

140. Patients with pulmonary stenosis have problems with obstruction of:

A. Left ventricular outflow

B. Right ventricular outflow

C. Left atrium outflow

D. Right ventricular outflow

Answer: B. Right ventricular outflow

Explanation: Patients with pulmonary stenosis have problems with obstruction of right ventricular outflow that causes right ventricular hypertrophy as the ventricle attempts to overcome resistance to the narrow valve.

141. Which method of evaluating an electrocardiogram reading involves estimating the heart rate by memorizing a sequence of numbers?

A. Times-ten method

B. 1,500 method

C. Sequence method

D. 1,200 method

Answer: C. Sequence method

Explanation: With the sequence method, the rate is determined by memorizing number sequences.

142. Which drug is used to decrease the risk of death post-MI, and also prevents the complications of prosthetic heart valves?

A. Fondoparinux

B. Heparin

C. Clopidogrel

D. Enoxaparin

Answer: A. Clopidogrel

Explanation: Clopidogrel (Plavix), Ticlopidine (Ticlid), Dipyridamole (Persantine), and Aspirin (Ecotrin) are used to decrease the risk of death post-MI, prevent complications of prosthetic heart valves, reduce risk of MI in patients with unstable MI, and prevent re-occlusion in coronary revascularization procedures.

143. Which endocrine disorder can cause premature atrial contractions (PACs)?

A. Hypothyroidism

B. Hyperthyroidism

C. Type II diabetes mellitus

D. Adrenal insufficiency

Answer: B. Hyperthyroidism

Explanation: PACs are associated with hyperthyroidism, hypoxia, acute respiratory failure, digoxin toxicity, electrolyte imbalances, coronary and vascular disease, and chronic pulmonary disease.

144. Which of the following drugs should be used in caution for the patient with asthma?

A. Flecainide

B. Lidocaine

C. Disopyramide

D. Mexilentine

Answer: C. Disopyramide

Explanation: Class 1A antiarrhythmic drugs (Disopyramide, Procainamide, and Quinidine) should be used cautiously in patients with asthma.

145. Nitrates work by:

A. Depressing the pacemaker activity of the SA node.

B. Dilating and relaxing the smooth muscle of the veins and arteries.

C. Slow conduction and refractory period of calcium-dependent tissues.

D. Suppress arrhythmias by converting a unidirectional block to a directional block.

Answer: B. Dilating and relaxing the smooth muscle of the veins and arteries.

Explanation: Nitrates are the drug of choice for acute angina and they work by dilating veins so less blood returns to the heart, thereby reducing the amount of blood in the ventricles at the end of diastole. This causes coronary artery dilation so more blood is delivered to the myocardium.

146. Which type of shock is characterized by massive vasodilation from loss or suppression of sympathetic tone, and it results from stress, anesthesia, or spinal cord injuries?

A. Anaphylactic shock

B. Neurogenic shock

C. Septic shock

D. Coronary shock

Answer: B. Neurogenic shock

Explanation: Anaphylactic shock is characterized by massive vasodilation and increased capillary permeability secondary to hypersensitivity reaction to an antigen. Septic shock is a form of severe sepsis, where there is hypotension and altered tissue perfusion. Neurogenic shock results in loss or suppression of sympathetic tone.

147. All of the following leg sites are at risk for embolism EXCEPT:

A. Femoral artery

B. Iliac artery

C. Popliteal artery

D. Sciatic artery

Answer: D. Sciatic artery

Explanation: There is a sciatic nerve of the posterior thigh. However, the three arteries where embolisms occur are the iliac, femoral, and popliteal arteries.

148. Complications of arterial occlusion include all of the following EXCEPT:

A. Skin ulceration

B. Impaired nail/hair growth

C. Stroke

D. Paralysis

Answer: Paralysis

Explanation: Complications of arterial occlusion include sever ischemia, necrosis, skin ulceration, gangrene, impaired nail/hair growth, stroke, TIA, and peripheral or systemic embolism.

149. Which diuretic can cause glucose levels to rise in diabetics?

A. Furosemide

B. Bumetanide

C. Ethacynic acid

D. Hydrochlorothiazide

Answer: D. Hydrochlorothiazide

Explanation: The thiazide diuretics are used to treat hypertension and edema, and the CV nurse must monitor glucose levels in diabetic patients.

150. Treatment of tricuspid stenosis includes:

A. Diuretics

B. Low sodium diet

C. Antiarrhythmic drugs

D. A and B

E. A, B, and C

Answer: D. A and B

Explanation: Treatment of tricuspid stenosis involves diuretics, low sodium diet, and surgery, if the stenosis is moderate to severe.

Exclusive Trivium Test Prep Test Tips and Study Strategies

Here at Trivium Test Prep, we strive to offer you the exemplary test tools that help you pass your exam the first time. This book includes an overview of important concepts, example questions throughout the text, and practice test questions. But we know that learning how to successfully take a test can be just as important as learning the content being tested. In addition to excelling on the CVN Exam we want to give you the solutions you need to be successful every time you take a test. Our study strategies, preparation pointers, and test tips will help you succeed as you take the CVN Exam and any test in the future!

Study Strategies

1. Spread out your studying. By taking the time to study a little bit every day, you strengthen your understanding of the testing material, so it's easier to recall that information on the day of the test. Our study guides make this easy by breaking up the concepts into sections with example practice questions, so you can test your knowledge as you read.

2. Create a study calendar. The sections of our book make it easy to review and practice with example questions on a schedule. Decide to read a specific number of pages or complete a number of practice questions every day. Breaking up all of the information in this way can make studying less overwhelming and more manageable.

3. Set measurable goals and motivational rewards. Follow your study calendar and reward yourself for completing reading, example questions, and practice problems and tests. You could take yourself out after a productive week of studying or watch a favorite show after reading a chapter. Treating yourself to rewards is a great way to stay motivated.

4. Use your current knowledge to understand new, unfamiliar concepts. When you learn something new, think about how it relates to something you know really well. Making connections between new ideas and your existing understanding can simplify the learning process and make the new information easier to remember.

5. Make learning interesting! If one aspect of a topic is interesting to you, it can make an entire concept easier to remember. Stay engaged and think about how concepts covered on the exam can affect the things you're interested in. The

sidebars throughout the text offer additional information that could make ideas easier to recall.

6. Find a study environment that works for you. For some people, absolute silence in a library results in the most effective study session, while others need the background noise of a coffee shop to fuel productive studying. There are many websites that generate white noise and recreate the sounds of different environments for studying. Figure out what distracts you and what engages you and plan accordingly.

7. Take practice tests in an environment that reflects the exam setting. While it's important to be as comfortable as possible when you study, practicing taking the test exactly as you'll take it on test day will make you more prepared for the actual exam. If your test starts on a Saturday morning, take your practice test on a Saturday morning. If you have access, try to find an empty classroom that has desks like the desks at testing center. The more closely you can mimic the testing center, the more prepared you'll feel on test day.

8. Study hard for the test in the days before the exam, but take it easy the night before and do something relaxing rather than studying and cramming. This will help decrease anxiety, allow you to get a better night's sleep, and be more mentally fresh during the big exam. Watch a light-hearted movie, read a favorite book, or take a walk, for example.

Preparation Pointers

1. Preparation is key! Don't wait until the day of your exam to gather your pencils, calculator, identification materials, or admission tickets. Check the requirements of the exam as soon as possible. Some tests require materials that may take more time to obtain, such as a passport-style photo, so be sure that you have plenty of time to collect everything. The night before the exam, lay out everything you'll need, so it's all ready to go on test day! We recommend at least two forms of ID, your admission ticket or confirmation, pencils, a high protein, compact snack, bottled water, and any necessary medications. Some testing centers will require you to put all of your supplies in a clear plastic bag. If you're prepared, you will be less stressed the morning of, and less likely to forget anything important.

2. If you're taking a pencil-and-paper exam, test your erasers on paper. Some erasers leave big, dark stains on paper instead of rubbing out pencil marks. Make sure your erasers work for you and the pencils you plan to use.

3. Make sure you give yourself your usual amount of sleep, preferably at least 7 – 8 hours. You may find you need even more sleep. Pay attention to how much you sleep in the days before the exam, and how many hours it takes for you to feel refreshed. This will allow you to be as sharp as possible during the test and make fewer simple mistakes.

4. Make sure to make transportation arrangements ahead of time, and have a backup plan in case your ride falls through. You don't want to be stressing about how you're going to get to the testing center the morning of the exam.

5. Many testing locations keep their air conditioners on high. You want to remember to bring a sweater or jacket in case the test center is too cold, as you never know how hot or cold the testing location could be. Remember, while you can always adjust for heat by removing layers, if you're cold, you're cold.

Test Tips

1. Go with your gut when choosing an answer. Statistically, the answer that comes to mind first is often the right one. This is assuming you studied the material, of course, which we hope you have done if you've read through one of our books!

2. For true or false questions: if you genuinely don't know the answer, mark it true. In most tests, there are typically more true answers than false answers.

3. For multiple-choice questions, read ALL the answer choices before marking an answer, even if you think you know the answer when you come across it. You may find your original "right" answer isn't necessarily the best option.

4. Look for key words: in multiple choice exams, particularly those that require you to read through a text, the questions typically contain key words. These key words can help the test taker choose the correct answer or confuse you if you don't recognize them. Common keywords are: *most, during, after, initially,* and *first.* Be sure you identify them before you read the available answers. Identifying the key words makes a huge difference in your chances of passing the test.

5. Narrow answers down by using the process of elimination: after you understand the question, read each answer. If you don't know the answer right away, use the process of elimination to narrow down the answer choices. It is easy to identify at least one answer that isn't correct. Continue to narrow down the choices before choosing the answer you believe best fits the question. By following this process, you increase your chances of selecting the correct answer.

6. Don't worry if others finish before or after you. Go at your own pace, and focus on the test in front of you.

7. Relax. With our help, we know you'll be ready to conquer the CVN Exam. You've studied and worked hard!

Keep in mind that every individual takes tests differently, so strategies that might work for you may not work for someone else. You know yourself best and are the best person to determine which of these tips and strategies will benefit your studying and test taking. Best of luck as you study, test, and work toward your future!

FREE DVD   **FREE DVD**

Essential Test Tips DVD from Trivium Test Prep!

Dear Customer,

Thank you for purchasing from Trivium Test Prep! We're honored to help you prepare for your exam.

To show our appreciation, we're offering a **FREE *Essential Test Tips* DVD by Trivium Test Prep**. Our DVD includes 35 test preparation strategies that will make you successful on your big exam. All we ask is that you email us your feedback and describe your experience with our product. Amazing, awful, or just so-so: we want to hear what you have to say!

To receive your **FREE *Essential Test Tips* DVD**, please email us at 5star@triviumtestprep.com. Include "Free 5 Star" in the subject line and the following information in your email:

1. The title of the product you purchased.

2. Your rating from 1 – 5 (with 5 being the best).

3. Your feedback about the product, including how our materials helped you meet your goals and ways in which we can improve our products.

4. Your full name and shipping address so we can send your **FREE *Essential Test Tips* DVD**.

If you have any questions or concerns please feel free to contact us directly at 5star@triviumtestprep.com. Thank you!

– Trivium Test Prep Team

CPSIA information can be obtained
at www.ICGtesting.com
Printed in the USA
BVHW061421081221
623451BV00007B/183